—HOW TO—
CHANGE
CAREERS

Beatryce Nivens

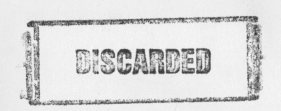
A PERIGEE BOOK

Perigee Books
are published by
The Putnam Publishing Group
200 Madison Avenue
New York, NY 10016

Library of Congress Cataloging-in-Publication Data

Nivens, Beatryce.
How to change careers / by Beatryce Nivens.
p.   cm. — (The Practical handbook series)
ISBN 0-399-51608-5
1. Career changes.   I. Title.
HF5384.N58   1990   89-48488   CIP
650.14—dc20

Printed in the United States of America

1 2 3 4 5 6 7 8 9 10

To the career women and men who think career changing
is a challenge rather than an obstacle. May you find happiness
in your new career.

Contents

Acknowledgments

The idea for *How to Change Careers* grew out of the many counseling sessions that I had with potential career changers. Most were frustrated, lost, and had no idea where to begin. All thought that they would have to get another degree or do something magical to change careers. After following the system that I designed for them, they found another way. By looking at themselves and designing their own job campaigns, they were able to successfully change careers. I thank them for their fortitude and energy.

To Adrienne Ingrum, my editor at Putnam's, who is one of my favorite people and one of the finest professionals in the publishing industry.

Sincere thanks to Carol Mann, my agent, who has been with me since the beginning. A chance meeting with her has turned into a beneficial relationship for both of us.

Great gratitude to Marilyn Ducksworth, who must be the greatest publicist in the world. She first looked at *How to Change Careers* in its infancy stages and suggested showing it to Adrienne. I shall always be grateful.

To Elza Dinwiddie-Boyd, who also suggested going to see Adrienne Ingrum. I shall always be grateful.

Yvonne Clear helped me put the original manuscript together. Without her assistance, this project could not have been completed. She went well beyond the scope of her job and proved that caring people are special.

I am truly grateful to Janine Coveney McAdams, who significantly enhanced this book with her feedback. Her love and support for the book is deeply appreciated.

Joanna Hardin, who typed the manuscript, is truly a gift from the universe. Her dedication to the project is deeply appreciated.

Many thanks to the professional associations (Professional Secretaries International, Convention Liaison Council) for their timely career information. Without their invaluable help, I would not have been able to complete this book. I also owe a great deal to the Department of Labor, Bureau of Labor Statistics, for their great book *The Dictionary of Occupational Titles*.

Special thanks to my family, who now know the demands writing can place upon a person.

Introduction

Are you burned out, tired, bored, underpaid, underemployed, and looking to get out of your present job? If so, you may want to change careers. Yet many of you may become frustrated with the career-changing process.

Each year thousands of men and women decide to change careers. Teachers, social workers, secretaries, administrative assistants, clerical workers, lawyers, nurses, accountants, bookkeepers, and others want to leave their present jobs and move into new, more exciting careers. Some will be forced to change because their companies have been merged or because of management streamlining. Still others will be the victims of company relocations: They can't or don't want to move.

In the past, many workers looked for secure jobs. They expected to find good jobs, remain until retirement, and get gold watches for twenty-five years of loyal service. But today, many workers can't simply remain in one secure job for a lifetime.

I have met hundreds of people who want to change careers. They truly want to better their lives and move into more challenging positions, yet many of them have no idea how to get started. Others have a good idea of what to do, but procrastinate for years. Many others just hope some magical person will do everything for them, or perhaps extraordinary circumstances will propel them into a new career.

In order to change careers, you must become active by getting involved in the process of landing a job in your chosen field. *How to Change Careers* will help you. You may decide to go back to school, but not before you've explored all options. If you have a high-school diploma, you will learn to transfer your work skills into new, challenging careers. If you're a college graduate, you won't have to do anything "magical" like getting a graduate degree or extensive training. In order for the system to work, however, you must be willing to say yes to taking an intensive look at yourself, your skills, and talents, and then be willing to act upon your findings.

In Chapter 1 you will learn how to set realistic goals. Most people just say, "I want to change careers." But what exactly do you want to do? What career do you want to change to? When do you want this to occur? What is the exact date? What will it take to make the career change and how long? One week? One month? One year or two years? Five years or more? You will learn the best ways used by successful people to set goals.

Chapter 2 helps get you in touch with your skills. You probably have hidden abilities that can help you successfully change careers, but without knowing what these are, you may be trapped by your job title and be underestimating your worth in the marketplace. You will learn how to write down all your skills by determining the ones you are using in your present and have used in past positions. You will even learn to recognize skills acquired in volunteer or civic or community work.

I have developed a "skills-analysis exercise" that will help you uncover many of your hidden abilities. In this chapter there are skills charts for the positions of secretary, teacher, social worker, nurse, administrative assistant, retail sales worker, and even for the nonpaid work experience of the fund-raiser. The techniques shown in these charts will also work for other types of jobs.

In Chapter 3 you will explore your work accomplishments: things you have done to contribute to the company where you work or ones for which you have worked in the past. What have you done to contribute to your company's sales, image, or efficiency? By looking at the work of the computer programmer; teacher; nurse; administrative assistant; real-estate salesperson; public-relations person and staffer, nonprofit agency; retail salesperson; trainer; and writer, you will learn how to determine your own work accomplishments.

By understanding these, you will be able to show a prospective employer that you are a worker who has accomplished things and contributed, and that you can transfer this same zeal to a new position.

Understanding your work accomplishments will make your résumé more marketable and give it impact. Imagine writing this accomplishment on your résumé: "Designed filing system that increased office efficiency by 60%," rather than "typed, filed, answered the phone." Or perhaps you can write, "Developed educational system to introduce inner-city students to the world of work that is now national model used by 300 school districts" instead of "taught 30 students." By knowing your work accomplishments, you can get a future employer to think, "If he or she did this for his or her present employer, maybe he or she can do this for us."

In Chapter 4, you will explore how to successfully move into another career. Chapter 4 lists careers that secretaries, teachers, nurses, lawyers, social workers, cosmetologists, and others can move into without getting more education. These are examples that you can apply to your own career change.

You will learn how to discover the skills needed for your new career and how to match yours to them. This will prepare you to write your résumé. And you will learn how to ask for a title change at your present position that will make it easier for you to change careers.

Chapter 5 helps you design a career-changing game plan. As a career changer, you will soon learn that some of the traditional job-hunting methods may not be the best for you. Want ads, employment agencies, or executive-recruitment firms, and state employment agencies may help you—or they may not.

You will discover how to control the job

search instead of giving that power to others. You will find out how to research your future industry or industries, or company or companies, and career area. You will understand the value of "fact-finding" interviews with people working in your future field to learn about it. You will learn how networking and joining professional associations can increase your chances for successful career moves.

After reading Chapter 6, résumé preparation will be easier for you. You will learn the three most popular types of résumé— chronological, functional, and combination, and why the functional and combination types are the best for career changers.

You will review all of your past paid and nonpaid positions to help you determine any experiences or skills that could be helpful in making a new career. This exercise is particularly important because we often forget many of our work experiences and what we learned from them.

In Chapter 6 you will learn step-by-step how to create your own career-changer's résumé. By examining the sample résumés you will learn how to write a powerful résumé for yourself.

Chapter 6 will also help you write a dynamic cover letter that will get results. By specifically highlighting your work experience, training, education, and other achieve-ments toward the position you want, you will be able to grab your future employer's attention.

Chapter 7 explores how to get through the much-dreaded, anxiety-provoking interview. You will learn the different types of interview situations and how to master them. You'll learn why practice interviews are important and how doing your career-changing homework will enable you to master interviews. You will discover ways to negotiate for a good salary.

Does the system contained in *How to Change Careers* work? Yes! Many of my clients have transferred their skills to new and better careers without having to return to school. Through this dynamic approach to career changing, many of them analyzed their marketable and transferable skills, set realistic goals, and successfully found new careers. With this empowering program, most of my clients were able to dramatically better their lives!

Will it take work and imagination? Yes! But a rewarding career is worth some energy and effort, for a little hard work and imagination may help you change from an ordinary job to an extraordinary career.

Beatryce Nivens
New York City

CHAPTER 1

Polishing Your Goals

What are goals and why are they important to you as a career changer? Goals are like little navigators that will keep you on course throughout your life. They will give you direction and help you get what you want. A person without goals is a person going nowhere. And, as a career changer, having goals will help you decide what you want to achieve, and when.

Take some quality or quiet time to decide what you want to do with the rest of your life. You may have to do some career homework investigating other fields to discover what you really want to do. (More about that in Chapter 5.) Or you may remember something you wanted to do a long time ago, but were discouraged by others from doing. Perhaps you can rediscover those original career dreams, clear away your doubts or other people's negative opinions, and pursue that field.

After you've spent your quality time determining what you really want to do, it's time to start setting some goals. You should have short-term goals (from right now until a year from now), medium-term goals (from one year to five years), and long-term goals (from five years until the end of your work life).

Let's say that you want to become a public-relations specialist. What would some of your short-, medium-, or long-term goals be? Let's look at Table 1 for some suggestions.

Now look at Table 2 and complete your own goal statement. Don't worry if you can't complete the medium-term or long-term goals in detail. Just estimate what you might like to do. The important thing is to really focus on your short-term goals and get started on them.

You will notice at the bottom of Table 2 that there are three sentences: (1) Date I want to accomplish my ultimate short-term goals, (2) Date I want to accomplish my ultimate medium-term goals, (3) Date I want to accomplish my ultimate long-term goals. Setting a date to accomplish your goals is an enormous help, for it makes them concrete. Many successful people have used this technique. It personally helped me to change my career from that of college counselor to writer despite tremendous odds. Each morning and evening I reviewed my goals out loud, for by repeating them I knew that I was impressing them on my subconscious mind and feeding the desire to achieve them. I carried on this

TABLE 1
Sample Goal-Statement Chart

My goal is to become a *Public-Relations Specialist*.

My short-term goals (from right now to one year from now):

A. *Learn more about the field.*

B. *Get an entry-level position in public relations at a company.*

How can I accomplish this?

a. Contact the Public Relations Society of America (the professional association in my future field) and ask for career information and books.

b. Read this information and also go to the library to get and read other career books about the field.

c. Try to join the Public Relations Society of America's local chapter in my area.

d. Go out on "fact-finding interviews" with people in my future field, starting with the lady in my church, Ann Graves, who owns a public-relations company.

   1. Contact Marvin Leese, whom I read about in our local newspaper. He is a corporate public-relations person at a local company.

   2. Contact Linda Jones, who is a public-relations person at St. John's Baptist Hospital.

   3. Talk to my cousin Marie, who works for a large company. She frequently has lunch with someone in the public-relations department.

   4. Talk to John's sister Katherine. She does free-lance public-relations work for small businesses.

   5. Ask each of these people for referrals to at least one other person.

e. Take course with local college's continuing education program called "The ABCs of Public Relations" (6 weeks).

f. Get list of public-relations companies from Chamber of Commerce.

g. Read as much as I can in newspapers, brochures, annual reports, magazines, books, about the companies.

h. Select three industries where I might want to work. Possibilities are cosmetics, fashion, or health fields.

   1. Research these industries.

   2. Start contacting companies and the people who can hire me.

i. Go on interviews.

Final Goal: GET ENTRY-LEVEL PUBLIC-RELATIONS POSITION

MEDIUM-TERM GOALS
(FROM ONE TO FIVE YEARS)

1. Begin making significant contributions to my new company.

2. Let my new boss know of my career plans, and keep him or her abreast of my new goals and contributions made to the company.

3. Take courses offered by new company that may help boost me up the ladder of success, i.e., "How to Manage Others"; "How to Manage Your Time."

4. Make myself visible within company.

5. Move into public-relations specialist slot anywhere from six months to one year after starting first position.

Final Goal: MANAGEMENT POSITION

LONG-TERM GOALS
(FROM FIVE YEARS UNTIL THE REST OF MY WORK LIFE)

Final Goal: TO BECOME VICE PRESIDENT OF PUBLIC RELATIONS

Ultimate Goal: TO OWN PUBLIC-RELATIONS FIRM DOING $1,000,000 OR MORE BUSINESS PER YEAR

Date I want to accomplish my ultimate short-term goals: *May 1, 1990*

Date I want to accomplish my ultimate medium-term goals: *December 31, 1993*

Date I want to accomplish my ultimate long-term goals: *December 31, 2000*

twice-daily ritual of reviewing and repeating my goals until my heart, mind, and soul believed I would succeed. What you believe, you can achieve! By writing down your goals, when you want to attain them, and repeating this until you truly desire it, you can successfully change careers. The key is to truly believe deep down inside that this is possible.

Another method you can use to help you

T A B L E 2
My Goal-Statement Chart

My goal is to become_____

_____

My Short-Term Goals
(From Right Now to One Year From Now)

A._____

B._____

How can I accomplish this?

a._____

b._____

c._____

d._____

e._____

f._____

g._____

h._____

i._____

j._____

k._____

l._____

*Final Goal:*_____

Medium-Term Goals
(From One Year to Five Years)

1._____

2._____

3._____

4._____

5._____

*Final Goal:*_____

T A B L E 2 (*Continued*)

Long-Term Goals
(From Five Years Until the Rest of My Work Life)

1._____

2._____

3._____

*Final Goal:*_____

*Ultimate Goal:*_____

Date I want to accomplish my ultimate short-term goals

_____

Date I want to accomplish my ultimate medium-term goals

_____

Date I want to accomplish my ultimate long-term goals

_____

change careers is to prepare a "desire book." This is a very well known procedure to help people visualize their success. Go to your local stationery store and purchase a regular 8½″ × 11″ notebook or picture album. Paste pictures in the book to depict your goals. Let's say you want to change from being a secretary to being a travel agent. Look through magazines and/or newspapers until you find pictures that depict the type of work you will be doing as a travel agent, or symbols of that work such as airplanes, cruise ships, or hotels.

Put a picture of yourself on the first page of your desire book. On the second page use another picture of yourself to show how you'll look in your new job. Will you wear a suit? Uniform? Costume? What equipment will you need at your new job? Will you be using a computer, adding machine, stenographic machine? Will you have your own office? Will you carry an attaché case? Put these things in the picture. Will you be working in, say, the cosmetics industry? Clip some pictures of cosmetics and put them in your book.

Include as many things as you can about your new position in your desire book. The new company name. Your salary. Be imaginative! The more characteristics you can come up with about your dream position, the better.

Now look at your desire book just after you wake up and before you go to bed. Start imagining yourself in your targeted position and really believe it will happen, that you will be there.

To keep in the proper state of mind every day, read books on positive thinking (see Appendix A) and listen to tapes on the subject. Books and tapes should be available at your bookstore or by mail order.

Another effective way to maintain a good mental attitude is to surround yourself with people who are positive, ones who won't be critical of your goals. There are plenty of such people in the world. Find them! You can go far if you have the encouragement of others.

Don't ever discuss your career goals with people who knock them and try to talk you out of them. Parents, mates, friends, relatives, and even casual acquaintances may try to "protect" you by putting down your dreams. Some do this out of genuine concern; others simply out of envy—fear that you will outdistance them someday. Others will criticize you just because they are by nature negative thinkers. They can't help it. So don't share your plans with them, and never listen to their "well-meaning" advice.

If you have goals and dreams, you can make them happen. It will take work and concentration, but if you follow the methods in this book, you will be successful. The secret is to believe that all things are possible—and get going on your trip to the top!

CHAPTER 2

Dazzle Yourself with Your Skills

Unfortunately, many people define themselves by their job titles. For example, you might say, "I'm a secretary" or "I'm a teacher." But if you actually defined yourself by your job duties, you would probably assume another job title. For example, a secretary might think of herself as just a secretary. But after looking at her job duties, she might discover that she is actually doing all the purchasing for her department. She is, in fact, a purchasing agent as well as a secretary.

Many people downplay their jobs. You are probably working well beyond your job title but you probably don't understand the true nature and scope of your job. As a result, you will be severely handicapped when you try to change careers.

I'll never forget a college job that I lost. I was being interviewed by a search committee for an administrative position at a local college. One member of the committee asked me, "Did you do any administrative work at your last job?" My response was no, because I defined myself by my previous job title: counselor. When the chairperson of the committee wrote me, he explained, "We were very impressed by you, but you didn't perform any administrative duties at your last job. We just couldn't take a chance. . . ."

Almost immediately I realized my mistake at that interview. My job title was counselor, but I had in fact done a great deal of administrative work. It just never occurred to me that managing a special program, overseeing a budget, and supervising others was administrative work; I simply thought of myself as "counselor." If I had defined myself as a counselor with administrative duties, I would have received a job offer.

In this chapter you will learn to get in touch with your "hidden job duties" by doing a skills-analysis exercise. Write down your job duties or what you do on a daily, weekly, or monthly basis at your job. Forget your job title! *Concentrate on what you do on a daily basis.* If you are unsure of this, make a daily, weekly, or monthly log that focuses on what you do during your workday.

Another way to determine your job duties is to think about your major responsibilities.

Let's take the example of a secretary whose major job duty is to supervise a pool of four typists. She is responsible for getting the typists to complete their assigned typing and then distributing the completed work to the appropriate managers. So, instead of being a "secretary," she is actually a supervisor.

Let's see what your job duties are. Take a piece of paper and draw a line down the middle. On the top left side of paper put "My Job Duties." On the top right side put "Skills Required."

Considering your major work responsibilities, or using your log as a guide, list your job duties on the left side of the paper. Now you are going to determine which skills are used to perform each duty. For example, the secretary whose major work responsibility is the supervision of four typists uses the following skills while performing this job duty:

- Establishes and maintains harmonious relationship with workers

- Analyzes best way to get assigned work completed

- Delegates work

- Manages others

- Sets deadlines

- Knows who will get the job done best

Table 3 is a list of over 250 skills. Use it to help you pinpoint the skills you use while performing your job duties.

To further help with your skills-analysis exercise, let's take the example of the receptionist. Everyone is familiar with this position and what it entails. One job duty of the receptionist is answering the phone. While doing so, what skills are being utilized? First, the receptionist must know how to communicate orally. Second, this man or woman is a "resource" expert who knows—or should know—where every employee is located and can be reached. Third, she or he must be able to screen incoming calls and take messages accurately. Fourth, the receptionist must have a pleasing manner and a lot of patience, for he or she is the ambassador, the goodwill representative for the company. A receptionist in some cases can make or break a company. Just think of the last time you called a company and were greeted with a snarl or your call was cut off. Did you want to do business with that firm again? Probably not.

Perhaps you thought that a receptionist has few if any skills. But through this exercise you have learned otherwise. If the receptionist has listed at least nine or more additional job duties, it means that he or she will have anywhere from fifty to one hundred different skills!

Look at the seven skills-analysis exercises for secretaries, teachers, social workers, nurses, lawyers, administrative assistants, and retail sales workers (Tables 4 through 10). Look at Table 4 to determine how to do these exercises. On the left side, the first job duty listed for a secretary is: "relieves executive of various administrative duties." On the right side, you will see "Skills Required." This means that in order to perform this one job duty, a secretary must use several skills. They are, in this case, "being of service to, being sensitive to boss, able to work under pressure," etc.

Table 11 is a skills-analysis exercise for a nonpaid, volunteer fund-raiser. We often do volunteer work and never consider it as marketable work experience. Since we aren't paid for our work, we assume it is valueless on the job market. No! Many women and men have used skills from nonpaid work to move into paid positions. So, when you are analyzing your past work skills, always include your nonpaid work. Don't forget any volunteer or civic work: fund-raiser, counselor, group leader, club officer, public-relations adviser, or whatever. Maybe you can parlay this experience into a better job!

TABLE 3
Skills List

____ 1. Abstracting	____ 45. Compiling	____ 90. Enduring
____ 2. Accommodating	____ 46. Composing	____ 91. Enforcing
____ 3. Accomplishing	____ 47. Computing	____ 92. Enlarging
____ 4. Accounting	____ 48. Conceiving	____ 93. Enlisting
____ 5. Acting	____ 49. Conducting	____ 94. Entertaining
____ 6. Activating	____ 50. Constructing	____ 95. Establishing
____ 7. Adapting	____ 51. Consulting	____ 96. Estimating
____ 8. Addressing	____ 52. Contacting	____ 97. Evaluating
____ 9. Adjusting	____ 53. Contributing	____ 98. Examining
____ 10. Administering	____ 54. Controlling	____ 99. Exercising
____ 11. Advertising	____ 55. Cooking	____100. Exhibiting
____ 12. Advising	____ 56. Cooperating	____101. Expanding
____ 13. Advocating	____ 57. Coordinating	____102. Expediting
____ 14. Allocating	____ 58. Copying	____103. Experimenting
____ 15. Analyzing	____ 59. Counseling	____104. Explaining
____ 16. Anticipating	____ 60. Counting	____105. Exploring
____ 17. Appraising	____ 61. Creating	____106. Expressing
____ 18. Approving	____ 62. Criticizing	____107. Facilitating
____ 19. Arranging	____ 63. Dancing	____108. Feeding
____ 20. Artistic ability	____ 64. Debating	____109. Filing
____ 21. Assembling	____ 65. Deciding	____110. Finding
____ 22. Asserting	____ 66. Decorating	____111. Fixing
____ 23. Assessing	____ 67. Defining	____112. Following
____ 24. Assigning	____ 68. Delegating	through
____ 25. Auditing	____ 69. Delivering	____113. Forecasting
____ 26. Balancing	____ 70. Demonstrating	____114. Formulating
____ 27. Bargaining	____ 71. Designing	____115. Fund raising
____ 28. Bookkeeping	____ 72. Detailing	____116. Gathering
____ 29. Brainstorming	____ 73. Detecting	____117. Governing
____ 30. Budgeting	____ 74. Determining	____118. Graphing
____ 31. Building	____ 75. Developing	____119. Group facilitating
____ 32. Calculating	____ 76. Devising	____120. Guiding
____ 33. Caring for	____ 77. Diagnosing	____121. Handling
____ 34. Cataloging	____ 78. Directing	____122. Handling
____ 35. Catering	____ 79. Disciplining	complaints
____ 36. Changing	____ 80. Discovering	____123. Handling details
____ 37. Classifying	____ 81. Discussing	____124. Hosting
____ 38. Coaching	____ 82. Dispensing	____125. Identifying
____ 39. Collaborating	____ 83. Displaying	____126. Imagining
____ 40. Collecting	____ 84. Distributing	____127. Implementing
____ 41. Combining	____ 85. Drafting	____128. Improving
____ 42. Committee	____ 86. Drawing	____129. Indexing
participation	____ 87. Editing	____130. Informing
____ 43. Communicating	____ 88. Educating	____131. Initiating
____ 44. Comparing	____ 89. Encouraging	____132. Innovating

T A B L E 3 (*continued*)

____133.	Inspecting	____175.	Painting	____220.	Risk-taking
____134.	Inspiring	____176.	Perceiving	____221.	Rewriting
____135.	Instructing	____177.	Performing	____222.	Scanning
____136.	Interpreting	____178.	Persevering	____223.	Scheduling
____137.	Interviewing	____179.	Persuading	____224.	Screening
____138.	Inventing	____180.	Planning	____225.	Self-motivating
____139.	Investigating	____181.	Policy making	____226.	Selling
____140.	Judging	____182.	Politicking	____227.	Taking shorthand
____141.	Justifying	____183.	Predicting	____228.	Simplifying
____142.	Laboratory skills	____184.	Preparing	____229.	Singing
____143.	Leading	____185.	Presenting	____230.	Solving
____144.	Learning	____186.	Presiding	____231.	Solving quantitative problems
____145.	Lecturing	____187.	Printing		
____146.	Listening	____188.	Prioritizing		
____147.	Lobbying	____189.	Problem solving	____232.	Stimulating
____148.	Locating	____190.	Processing	____233.	Strategizing
____149.	Making layouts	____191.	Producing	____234.	Strengthening
____150.	Making models	____192.	Programming	____235.	Summarizing
____151.	Maintaining	____193.	Promoting	____236.	Supervising
____152.	Managing	____194.	Proofreading	____237.	Systematizing
____153.	Manipulating	____195.	Proposing	____238.	Talking
____154.	Mapping	____196.	Protecting	____239.	Targeting
____155.	Measuring	____197.	Public speaking	____240.	Teaching
____156.	Mechanical reasoning	____198.	Purchasing	____241.	Team building
		____199.	Reacting	____242.	Technical ability
____157.	Mediating	____200.	Reading	____243.	Thinking
____158.	Meeting the public	____201.	Reasoning	____244.	Timing
		____202.	Recognizing problems	____245.	Training
____159.	Memorizing			____246.	Transmitting
____160.	Moderating	____203.	Recommending	____247.	Treating
____161.	Modifying	____204.	Reconciling	____248.	Troubleshooting
____162.	Monitoring	____205.	Recording	____249.	Typing
____163.	Motivating	____206.	Record keeping	____250.	Understanding
____164.	Moving with dexterity	____207.	Recruiting	____251.	Updating
		____208.	Rectifying	____252.	Using instruments
____165.	Navigating	____209.	Reducing costs		
____166.	Negotiating	____210.	Rehabilitating	____253.	Utilizing
____167.	Nursing	____211.	Remembering	____254.	Validating
____168.	Observing	____212.	Reorganizing	____255.	Visualizing
____169.	Obtaining information	____213.	Reporting	____256.	Working with others
		____214.	Representing		
____170.	Operating	____215.	Reproducing	____257.	Working with precision
____171.	Ordering	____216.	Researching		
____172.	Orderliness	____217.	Resolving	____258.	Writing
____173.	Organizing	____218.	Restoring		
____174.	Overseeing	____219.	Reviewing		

TABLE 4*
Skills Analysis: Secretaries

DUTIES	SKILLS REQUIRED
1. Relieves executive of various administrative duties.	1. Being of service to, being sensitive to boss, able to work under pressure, etc.
2. Coordinates and maintains effective office procedures and efficient workflow.	2. Gets the job done, has ability to motivate others to get the job done, able to persuade, able to facilitate.
3. Implements policies and procedures set by employers.	3. Is orderly, keeps records, able to process information, can do many tasks.
4. Establishes and maintains harmonious working relationships with superiors, co-workers, subordinates, customers or clients, and suppliers.	4. Takes initative, has people-management skills, relates well to public and fellow employees/boss, has ability to effectively deal with many people.
5. Schedules appointments and maintains calendar.	5. Coordinates, able to persuade when difficulty arises, able to evaluate.
6. Receives and assists visitors and telephone callers and refers them to executive.	6. Has diplomacy skills, sensitivity to others, is patient and fair, is comfortable with many different kinds of people.
7. Arranges business itineraries and coordinates executive travel requirements.	7. Is helpful, good at organizing details and written material, makes arrangements for others, is responsible.
8. Takes action authorized during executive's absence, and uses initiative and judgment to see that matters requiring attention are referred to delegated authority or handles in a manner so as to minimize effect of employer's absence.	8. Able to follow through, able to assist and lead in absence of boss, able to assume other duties, able to direct others, able to communicate effectively.
9. Takes manual shorthand and transcribes from it or transcribes from machine dictation.	9. Takes shorthand. Able to transcribe.
10. Types material from longhand or rough copy.	10. Types, analyzes, edits, corrects, and obtains information from boss or others to complete the job.
11. Sorts and reads incoming mail and documents and attaches appropriate file to faciliate necessary action.	11. Able to sort, read, file and observe. Gets the task done. Able to do follow-up and detail work.
12. Composes correspondence and reports for own or executive signature.	12. Writes well, able to compose letters.
13. Prepares communication outlined by executive in oral or written directions.	13. Able to follow directions.

*Source: *Prototype Secretarial Job Description,* Copyright © 1978, Professional Secretaries International. Reprinted with permission. Source for duties: *Dictionary of Occupational Titles,* Department of Labor, Bureau of Labor Statistics. Table from *The Black Woman's Career Guide,* by Beatryce Nivens. Copyright © 1982, 1987 by Beatryce Nivens. Used by permission of Doubleday, a division of Bantam Doubleday Dell Publishing Group, Inc.

T A B L E 5*

Skills Analysis: Teachers

DUTIES	SKILLS REQUIRED
1. Trains.	1. Able to talk in front of group. Teaching. Able to persuade. Able to promote your idea. Can lead. Able to design programs. Can guide.
2. Knowledgeable of curriculum guides and learning resources.	2. Able to read and digest materials. Has the ability to summarize. Able to review and evaluate. Able to know what interests others.
3. Sets objectives.	3. Able to work on own with little or no supervision. Plans. Researches. Makes priorities.
4. Plans classroom activities and makes assessment of the success of instruction.	4. Plans. Good at organizing. Able to carry out plans. Keeps record of progress. Able to review, evaluate and judge.
5. Motivates and stimulates students.	5. Able to influence others. Is sensitive to others. Creates an environment for learning and intellectual exchange.
6. Helps children become aware of their self-worth.	6. Able to establish good rapport. Able to show others their self-worth. Able to dig deep to help people know themselves. Able to design activities to help others determine their self-worth.
7. Expands and develops students' abilities.	7. Able to develop. Able to look at situations and people and decide which activities and materials might help them advance. Able to appraise and move on. Able to size up people and create alternatives to speed up progress.
8. Analyzes students' grades to determine progress.	8. Can determine, analyze, and diagnose.
9. Proficient in the basic skills of particular subject.	9. Able to read, write and do math. Proficient in particular subject area, such as language (Spanish, French), music, art, home economics, etc.
10. Creative and innovative in projects.	10. Imaginative, good at coming up with original projects. Good at drawing and putting things together. Good at getting the job done.

T A B L E 5* (continued)

DUTIES	SKILLS REQUIRED
11. Develops interpersonal relationships.	11. Able to help others. Able to talk things through. Able to command respect. Can help people work better together. Can help people cope with school and others.
12. Develops testing methods.	12. Is creative. Able to determine the needs of others and translate this into methods which are most conducive to learning. Able to develop tests. Able to predict whether others can adapt their learning to which tests. Able to conceptualize.
13. Interprets tests and reports to parents or students.	13. Able to interpret tests and translate these results into meaningful analysis for students and parents. Good communication skills, both in writing and speaking. Able to tactfully explain results. Able to deal with potentially sticky situations.
14. Reads and prepares materials.	14. Able to read, interpret, and analyze.
15. Makes referrals.	15. Able to size up situations and act in the best interest of another. Able to get all of the facts and make an assessment. Able to be fair. Has negotiating skills. Is persuasive.
16. Plans classroom activities and makes assessment of the success of instruction.	16. Is diplomatic. Sensitive. Has ability to get others to do what you want. Good at problem solving.
17. Knows how to work with young children, adolescents or young adults.	17. Good people-management skills. Knows how to get younger people to work effectively with each other.
18. Knows how to organize time.	18. Has good time-management skills. Good at organizing. Able to get job done.

* Source for duties: *Dictionary of Occupational Titles,* Department of Labor, Bureau of Labor Statistics. Table from *The Black Woman's Career Guide,* by Beatryce Nivens. Copyright © 1982, 1987 by Beatryce Nivens. Used by permission of Doubleday, a division of Bantam Doubleday Dell Publishing Group, Inc.

T A B L E 6*
Skills Analysis: Social Workers

DUTIES	SKILLS REQUIRED
1. Interviews.	1. Develops rapport and trust, keeps confidences or confidential information, has good verbal/communications skills, able to encourage communication.
2. Assesses clients needs.	2. Sensitive to others, remembers people and their preferences, understands human motivations, can appraise, can size up situations and understands political realities.
3. Arranges for services, i.e., food stamps, medical care, educational opportunities.	3. Able to locate resources, can make and use contacts effectively, good at compiling, skilled at clarifying problems or situations, adept at gathering information, analyzing and processing information, is organized and orderly, good at keeping track of information, collects data accurately.
4. Keeps records.	4. Has keen and accurate memory for details, keeps track of information, has high tolerance for repetition or monototony, collects data accurately.
5. Is an advocate for clients.	5. Serves as a change agent, can promote another individual, leads others, inspires by bringing people together in cooperative efforts, renders service to others, treats people fairly, has unusual ability to represent others.
6. Has good listening skills.	6. Has accurate hearing. Determines, evaluates, diagnoses, is perceptive, treats others as equals.
7. Provides placement services.	7. Able to assess, appraise and screen another's needs and feelings, able to match personal needs with resources and jobs, able to develop warmth over the telephone.
8. Creates programs.	8. Plans, develops, has systematic approach to goal setting, formulates policy, interprets, good at program development.
9. Evaluates.	9. Revises, analyzes, makes recommendations, makes good use of feedback, able to judge.

T A B L E 6* (continued)

DUTIES	SKILLS REQUIRED
10. Empowers others.	10. Helps people identify their own intelligence, encourages and motivates others; able to raise people's self esteem, able to help others express their views.
11. Has administrative and leadership skills.	11. Able to take charge, able to work alone, able to organize others and bring people together in cooperative efforts, schedules, assigns, coordinates operations and details, directs others, makes decisions about others, takes initiative, excellent at organizing time, shows courage, serves as role model.
12. Informs.	12. Communicates well, makes assessments, adept at two-way conversation.
13. Handles and manages unexpected or unpleasant stress.	13. Able to ignore undesirable qualities in others, can deal patiently, sympathetically with difficult people.
14. Possesses sensitivity, empathy and diplomacy.	14. Relates well to people, is intuitive, establishes rapport/trust, is warm and responsive to other's needs.
15. Has good writing and oral skills.	15. Has good communications and organizational skills, clear in thought, able to communicate for self and others.
16. Thinks critically.	16. Analyzes, reviews, and evaluates information, makes decisions, diagnoses, solves problems.
17. Acts objectively.	17. Able to act in unbiased manner, can validate information.
18. Counsels.	18. Sensitive to other's needs, able to mediate between conflicting parties, advocates, shows caring and warmth, able to act in best interest of others, able to help others act for themselves.

* Source for duties: *Dictionary of Occupational Titles*, Department of Labor, Bureau of Labor Statistics. Table from *The Black Woman's Career Guide*, by Beatryce Nivens. Copyright © 1982, 1987 by Beatryce Nivens. Used by permission of Doubleday, a division of Bantam Doubleday Dell Publishing Group, Inc.

TABLE 7*
Skills Analysis: Nurses

DUTIES	SKILLS REQUIRED
1. Has medical and health-care knowledge. Keeps up with developments in the industry.	1. Is good at analyzing and understanding data; can evaluate materials; can explain material; is good at obtaining material; can process information; can review information.
2. Renders general nursing care to patients in hospitals, infirmaries, sanitariums or similar institutions.	2. Can examine; can appraise situation; can arrange for the best care; can coordinate nursing care; can work under pressure; can make decisions; can review and evaluate; is good at dealing with the public; can handle complaints.
3. Has knowledge of and administers prescribed medications and treatments in accordance with approved nursing techniques.	3. Knows how to inspect to make sure right medication and treatment are given; is good at observing; is organized; is able to calm patients; can work with different people.
4. Prepares equipment and aids physician during treatment and examination of patients.	4. Knows and understands nature of equipment; can assist physician; is able to work under supervision; is observant; can monitor and operate equipment.
5. Prepares patient for and assists with examinations; observes patient; records significant reactions and notifies supervisor or physician of patients' condition and reaction to drugs, treatments and significant incidents.	5. Able to counsel and comfort; can observe problems with patient; can remember details for doctor; able to record details; can work with others; can advise physician of observations.
6. Checks temperature, pulse, blood pressure and other vital signs to detect deviations from normal and determine progress of patient.	6. Able to take care of others; can record findings; can determine what findings mean; has knowledge of what various indicators mean.
7. May make beds, bathe, and feed patients, and assist in their rehabilitation.	7. Knows careful and correct methods of bathing and feeding patients; can talk to and help patients recover.
8. May act as a receptionist, performing secretarial duties and prepare monthly statements.	8. Can perform general clerical duties; is physician's office ambassador; is courteous and helpful to public; may know how to type and perform simple bookkeeping tasks; understands health insurance forms and how to fill them out.

* Source for duties: *Dictionary of Occupational Titles,* Department of Labor, Bureau of Labor Statistics.

TABLE 8*

Skills Analysis: Lawyers
(Corporate, Patent, Criminal, Etc.)

DUTIES	SKILLS REQUIRED
1. Advises clients concerning legal rights, obligations, and privileges.	1. Able to communicate well orally and in writing; able to address needs; can analyze; good at appraising; can assess; able to collect information; can make recommendations; able to consult; good at cooperating; can discuss important matters; is encouraging; can evaluate; able to explain; can investigate; able to counsel; is good observer; can obtain information; good at organizing; good at public speaking; good at representing; able to study constitution, statutes, decisions and ordinances.
2. Examines legal data to determine advisability of defending or prosecuting lawsuit.	2. Able to make determinations; good at researching; is good problem-solver; able to identify problem areas; able to explore; is good with details; good at advising.
3. May act as agent of client in various transactions.	3. Able to represent; may mediate; is persuasive; can make good decisions; is troubleshooter; can handle complaints; good at following through; is an initiator; able to interview others; can meet the public; good at negotiating; can present material to others; able to promote; can resolve problems; can make recommendations.
4. Conducts criminal and civil lawsuits.	4. Able to gather and analyze evidence; able to delegate; can review evidence; good at obtaining information; able to plan; good at investigating; can formulate theories; can direct others.
5. Draws up legal documents.	5. Knows legal terminology; can write well; able to locate resources to help; is disciplined; able to work alone for long hours; has good concentration; is good at details; able to compile information; can interpret law.
6. Advises clients as to legal rights.	6. Can predict outcome; able to counsel; good at handling complaints; can evaluate; able to discuss; able to consult; has good listening skills.

T A B L E 8* (continued)

DUTIES	SKILLS REQUIRED
7. Represents clients.	7. Is advocate for clients; protects clients; knows how to prepare client for trial; makes good decisions; able to care for others; able to control situation; can debate; can console; can make justifications; is a good leader; is inspiring; is able to motivate; can educate; able to get others to see both sides.
8. Presents evidence on behalf of client or against the accused.	8. Has good observation skills; good at filing; able to edit; can prepare exhibit materials; can examine; able to collect evidence.

* Source for duties: *Dictionary of Occupational Titles,* Department of Labor, Bureau of Labor Statistics.

TABLE 9*
Skills Analysis: Administrative Assistants

DUTIES	SKILLS REQUIRED
1. Aids executive by coordinating office services such as personnel and budget preparation and control.	1. Is of service to boss; is organized; able to appraise services; plans effectively; can delegate tasks; can do detail work; can initiate; able to manage information and people; is able to obtain information; monitors; able to keep records; can formulate budgets.
2. Studies management methods in order to improve workflow; simplifies reporting procedures or implements cost reductions; analyzes unit operating practices such as record-keeping systems; forms control, office layout, suggestion systems, personnel and budgetary requirements and performance standards to create new systems or revise established procedures.	2. Appraises and evaluates office setup; researches; investigates; obtains statistical data; determines most effective systems to increase office efficiency; designs plan of action; estimates cost of operation; prepares findings for boss; makes recommendations; advises.
3. Analyzes jobs to define position responsibilities for use in wage and salary adjustments.	3. Reviews and interprets duties for various jobs; classifies; makes decisions about job; examines; estimates salaries; does detail work; does record keeping; is resourceful; updates and improves.
4. Coordinates collection and preparation of operating reports such as time and attendance records, terminations, new hires, transfers, budget expenditures and statistical records of performance data.	4. Supervises; advises others; compiles statistical information; designs plan that will implement action; explains procedures to others; finds others who can be helpful to project; able to locate information; is responsible for getting the work done; motivates others to get the job done; able to persuade.
5. Prepares reports including conclusions and recommendations.	5. Able to write; able to review; analyzes data; interprets and advises in writing to others; observes; reports; compares; summarizes; make recommendations; able to collect information, compile and put into a report; makes decisions; able to deal with deadlines and pressure; initiates new ideas.
6. Issues and interprets operating policies.	6. Reviews; able to orally communicate; able to define; able to give directions to others; reports on policies; able to advise; able to explain; able to interpret; able to persuade; represents boss to other employees; able to teach.

T A B L E 9* (continued)

DUTIES	SKILLS REQUIRED
7. Reviews and answers correspondence.	7. Communicates effectively through writing; able to observe; able to initiate letters; able to edit; able to prioritize; able to make decisions; evaluates; able to express thoughts in writing.
8. May interview job applicants; direct orientation of new employees.	8. Recruits; able to screen; able to listen; can make decisions; able to obtain information; able to observe; able to choose; able to coach; teaches; able to influence others.
9. May direct services, such as maintenance.	9. Able to supervise; able to make others get the job done; can appraise; can make decisions; able to observe others in the process of performing work tasks.

* Source for duties: *Dictionary of Occupational Titles,* Department of Labor, Bureau of Labor Statistics. This material first appeared in *Careers for Women Without College Degrees* by Beatryce Nivens. Copyright © 1988 by Beatryce Nivens. Used by permission of McGraw-Hill Book Company.

TABLE 10*
Skills Analysis: Retail Sales Workers

DUTIES	SKILLS REQUIRED
1. Obtains merchandise; totals bills; receives payment; makes change for customers.	1. Able to select or choose; able to sell; is of service to, able to deal with the public; is diplomatic; is enthusiastic; uses good judgment; has integrity; able to communicate; able to close a deal; can calculate; can do simple mathematical equations; can collect; able to persuade.
2. Stocks shelves, counters, or tables with merchandise.	2. Able to inspect and compare; able to classify; can make decisions; able to locate; able to handle detail work; can organize; able to do inventory.
3. Sets up advertising displays or arranges merchandise on counters or tables to promote sales.	3. Able to do design; can predict; able to promote; can sell; able to persuade and stimulate; able to create displays based on correct colors, shapes, and products; is visual.
4. Stamps, marks, or tags prices on merchandise.	4. Able to use marking devices; inspects; able to work at a fast pace; pays attention to detail; able to be persistent; can sort; able to deal with pressure; locates; can observe.
5. Obtains merchandise requested by customers or receives merchandise selected by customers.	5. Able to sell; can distribute; able to get the job done; able to follow through; good at listening; can handle difficult people; able to deal with pressure; able to handle complaints.
6. Totals price and tax on merchandise selected by customers using paper and pencil, cash register, or adding machine to determine bill; receives payment and makes change.	6. Able to calculate; can add and subtract; able to use the cash register or adding machine; can count; able to represent employer to the public; able to determine and decide; can collect.
7. May calculate sales discount in preparing sales slip.	7. Able to do simple mathematics; able to decide feasibility of discount; able to advise supervisor of discount; has listening skills.
8. Wraps or bags merchandise for customers.	8. Able to fold or pack correctly; is patient; pays attention to detail.
9. May keep record of sales, prepare inventory of stock or order merchandise.	9. Able to do record keeping; able to log information; keeps files and/or file system; able to estimate; can make decisions; able to inspect; can take orders.

T A B L E 11*
Skills Analysis: Fund-Raiser
(Nonpaid Work)

DUTIES	SKILLS REQUIRED
1. Plans fund-raising program for charities or other causes.	1. Analyzes situation; anticipates problems and prepares for possible solutions; sets goals and objectives; calculates costs; works with committee to plan program.
2. Writes to, telephones, or visits individuals or establishments to solicit funds. Persuades them to contribute funds by explaining purpose and benefits of fund-raising program.	2. Is diplomatic; is persuasive; is good at explaining; can sell program to others; can coordinate; is good at organizing oneself; can dramatize plight; knows time management principles; can deal with negative feedback or difficult people; can endure long hours of work; is able to deal with public; can advise.
3. Compiles and analyzes information about potential customers to develop mailing or contact list and to plan selling approach.	3. Can classify information; understands target population; can use computer to develop mailing list; can coordinate; can create list; can make decisions; can do detail work; can investigate; can obtain information; can record; can do research.
4. Takes pledges or funds from contributors.	4. Can arrange for collection; can deal with pressure; can count or make sure correct money is collected; is courteous; is appreciative; is good at observing.
5. Records expenses incurred and contributions received.	5. Can do record keeping; can compile; can protect money; can review; can collect; can examine.
6. May organize volunteers and plan social functions to raise funds.	6. Can supervise others; can get others to get the job done; can make budget and calculate costs for function; can recruit performers or workers for event; can negotiate with facility that will house function; able to get people to attend function.
7. May prepare fund-raising brochures for mail solicitation program.	7. Knows how to write copy; makes decision of what brochure copy will say and hires writer; understands direct-mail procedures; calculates costs.

* Source for duties: *Dictionary of Occupational Titles*, Department of Labor, Bureau of Labor Statistics.

CHAPTER 3

Honing Your Work Accomplishments

In order to successfully change careers, you must convince your future employer that you (1) can do the work required by your new position and (2) will make a contribution to the company or organization. One of the best ways to do this is to show your future boss your work accomplishments from your present and other jobs. When strategically placed on a résumé, these accomplishments will get results.

What are work accomplishments? They are things that you have done to improve your company or organization. Ask yourself: What have I done to increase sales for my company or organization? What have I done to save time for it? What extra things have I done that have improved my job efficiency or gone beyond my job title?

In Chapter 2, "Dazzle Yourself with Your Skills," you probably found that you are doing more at your job than your job title indicates. This is good, and will help you with the career change. But now you must discover your work accomplishments. Knowing them will help strengthen your career move.

Let me give you an example. A woman was a secretary for a business school. One of her job duties was filing student folders. Before she came to work there, instructors and administrators would waste hours looking for a folder in the clutter of the filing room. Things were disorganized, and there was no rhyme or reason for how folders were filed. People even left folders on top of filing cabinets after looking through them.

The place was a mess, and this slowed productivity. This bright secretary decided to do something about it. First she organized the files into "active" and "inactive" students. Then she devised a system in which students in each program would be identified by a color code. For instance, if an instructor in word processing wanted to retrieve a folder for a student in her class, she would immediately go to the red-coded folders. This made things so easy that people could pull folders and put them back in less than half the time.

Although the secretary saved her organization wasted time and energy by reducing file-retrieval time by about 60%, she failed to see this as an accomplishment, and when it was time to change careers, she listed her job duties on the résumé as "file, type, answer the phone." If she had realized the extent of her work accomplishments, she would have written one job duty as "designed filing system that increased office efficiency by 60%." She would have had a much better chance of changing careers with this information on her résumé.

You have a better chance at successful career changing when you chronicle your work accomplishments. This will show your future boss in black and white that you aren't just an ordinary employee. Your accomplishments will say to your new boss that you went beyond the parameters of your job description, and that you can do the same for his or her company.

How do you determine your work accomplishments? Think back to when you began your present job. Are there things you did that made you proud? Perhaps you did something for your department that no one noticed. Maybe you didn't even get a thank you, but it was something that made you happy or satisfied. That is probably a work accomplishment.

A bookkeeping clerk listed his accomplishments like this:

- Prepared monthly payrolls ($250,000) for twenty clients.

- Increased client retention by 65% as a result of innovative accounting systems.

- Brought in ten new clients (accounts totaling $75,000) to firm because of reputation for handling other clients.

- Developed and instituted new accounting system from manual one, which increased efficiency by 80%.

- Designed "Maximum System" to help solve accounts-payable problems promptly. System decreased accounts-payable problems by 50%.

To help you determine your work accomplishments, look at Table 12: the work accomplishments of a computer programmer; teacher; nurse; public-relations specialist; real-estate salesperson; administrative assistant; staffer, nonprofit agency; retail salesperson; trainer; and writer. From looking at these examples, try to determine your work accomplishments.

Now that you have defined your work accomplishments, you are ready to utilize them to lay the foundation for your career change. Your work accomplishments will help you write your résumé (see Chapter 6).

They will also help you position yourself for a career change. As I mentioned, many career changers are trapped by their job titles, which makes it difficult for them to cross over to a higher-level job. Take the case of an administrative assistant who wants to be a meeting planner. In her present position she is performing many of a meeting planner's duties, but her title is administrative assistant. Perhaps her boss doesn't even realize that she is the meeting planner for the department.

For the sake of the future, this career changer must do two things: (1) make her boss aware of what she does on a daily basis; (2) request a title change that includes *everything* she really does. It will be much better for this person to go out into the job market with the title of "assistant meeting planner," or "special assistant in charge of meeting planning," or "administrative assistant/ meeting planner," rather than just "administrative assistant."

TABLE 12
Work Accomplishments

Computer Programmer: Researched, designed, and wrote cost-effective program for accounting department's payroll system. Saved company $45,000 by increasing department's efficiency and reducing payroll errors.

Teacher: Wrote and designed career program to introduce inner-city students to the "world of work." Program generated $100,000 in corporate contributions and is now national model for other school districts.

Nurse: Designed training program for new nurses to teach operational and personnel procedures. Resulted in saving hospital $10,000 in costly operational errors.

Public-Relations Specialist: Designed successful public-relations campaign for company president. More than 200 local and national newspapers wrote articles about president. As result, was rewarded United Press International (UPI) Award.

Real-Estate Salesperson: Sold $13.5 million in commercial real estate in six months.

Administrative Assistant: Saved company $17,000–$20,000 annually by developing office-efficiency system that reduced costly secretarial errors.

Staffer, Nonprofit Agency: Wrote proposal to implement in-house employment-placement component that saved organization $1 million in outside consultant fees.

Retail Salesperson: Increased department annual sales from $40,000 to $150,000 by creating "disco" environment on floor.

Trainer: Designed and led training workshop on "time management" which increased productivity of trainees by 65%.

Writer: Wrote two books that sold over 50,000 copies each because of unique marketing strategy.

If you are in a similar predicament, or just need a better title, make a list of your work accomplishments and let your boss know about them in a formal meeting. Don't make the assumption that your boss knows what you are doing on a daily basis. It's up to you to make it known.

After you have outlined your accomplishments, get your boss to acknowledge them and then ask for a new title. For example, you might say, "Don, as you see, I'm really doing the work of a meeting planner. I think my title should reflect the work that I'm actually doing."

Next, discuss your career plans for the company you are now with. You are setting the stage for getting a title change. Just say something like this: "I really like the meeting-planning aspects of my position. I've joined the professional association in the field and plan to get certified through its training component." This will show your boss that you are interested in your career and are trying to grow professionally. This should also strengthen your case to get a title change.

Title changes are usually easier to get than promotions or raises. You are simply asking your boss to give you a title that reflects what you do on a daily basis. You are not asking to be moved up the corporate or organizational ladder, and you are not trying to pry any money from the company's coffers.

Although you may be reluctant to ask for a title change, and probably can think of a million reasons why you won't get one, try to do it. Finding the nerve to ask for something is the hardest part. The important thing to remember is that you must ask.

Suppose your boss says that he or she can't help you. Find out why. You aren't asking for money, so it can't be a budgetary consideration. So why the refusal? If she or he says that this has never been done before, have your facts and figures ready. Say, for example, "Tim Jones was given the title of program supervisor even though that title had never existed before. His boss just wanted to reflect the work he was doing on a daily basis."

If your boss says that she or he will feel more comfortable giving you the new title after you have certification in the field or have taken a course or two, ask them for their word on this, and do what was requested. Then return and request the promised title change.

Not all bosses will agree to the request, so you may have to put up with a restrictive job title for a while. In that case, emphasize your list of work achievements on your résumé and stress to your future employer that your title does not give you full credit for what you do.

Or you can use the functional résumé (see Chapter 6) to highlight the skills needed for your future position. In this way you can de-emphasize your job title and concentrate on your skills and work accomplishments.

CHAPTER 4

Moving into New Careers without Getting More Education

Many frustrated career changers believe that earning a college degree or graduate degree such as an MBA (Master of Business Administration), JD (Doctor of Jurisprudence), or MPA (Master of Public Administration) will get them a better-paying job. Depending on your career goals, you *may* need additional training to fulfill your dreams. Most of you, however, won't have to return to school to successfully change careers. There are plenty of jobs you can land with only your present skills and experience. The trick is knowing exactly what your skills and marketable experience consist of.

Now that you have completed your skills-analysis exercise, you have a list of all your current skills that could be transferred to another field. But which field should you transfer to? To make this decision, you must determine the skills demanded by your future career. For example, look at Table 13. On the left you'll see a list of skills used by meeting planners. If you are interested in becoming a meeting planner, you should match your skills to the ones listed in Table 13.

If you are interested in other careers, look up the skills used by professionals in these fields in *The Dictionary of Occupational Titles* (Department of Labor, Bureau of Labor Statistics), which can be found in local libraries. Career books can also be helpful.

Next, you'll want to know which careers you can directly transfer your skills to. In Tables 14–19 you'll learn the best careers to which people in various fields can transfer. These charts take into consideration the skills used in your various positions and their transferability. For example, a nurse has skills that include "knowledge of the medical and health field; knowledge of prescribed medications and treatments; caring for others; supervision of others—LPNs, nurses' aides, orderlies; working under pressure; counseling the sick and their relatives; working with salespeople (pharmaceutical, medical and hospital supply, etc.). So a nurse who wants to change careers might transfer these skills to pharmaceutical or medical and hospital sales, corporate health-program management, or health education among other possibilities.

Use these tables as a starting point to help you match your skills with those of your desired career.

39

TABLE 13*

Matching Skills That I Have for the Job I Want

SKILLS NEEDED FOR MY FUTURE CAREER AS MEETING PLANNER	MATCHING SKILLS THAT I HAVE
1. Establishing meeting design and objectives.	1. _____
2. Selecting site and facilities.	2. _____
3. Negotiating with facilities.	3. _____
4. Budgeting.	4. _____
5. Handling reservations and housing.	5. _____
6. Choosing from transportation and housing.	6. _____
7. Planning program.	7. _____
8. Planning guidebook/staging guide documentation of specification.	8. _____
9. Establishing registration procedures.	9. _____
10. Arranging for and using support services, convention bureau, or outside services hospitality committee.	10. _____
11. Coordinating with convention center and hall.	11. _____
12. Planning with convention service manager.	12. _____
13. Briefing facilities staff (pre-meeting).	13. _____
14. Shipping.	14. _____
15. Planning function-rooms setup.	15. _____
16. Managing exhibits.	16. _____
17. Managing food and beverage.	17. _____
18. Determining audiovisual requirements.	18. _____
19. Selecting speakers.	19. _____
20. Booking entertainment.	20. _____
21. Scheduling promotion and publicity.	21. _____
22. Developing guest and family programs.	22. _____
23. Producing and printing meeting materials.	23. _____
24. Distributing gratuities.	24. _____
25. Evaluating (post-meeting).	25. _____

* Source: Convention Liaison Council, 1575 (I) Eye Street, Suite 1200, Washington, DC 20005. Reprinted with permission.

TABLE 14
Careers Secretaries Can Transfer To:

- Real-estate agent
- Travel agent
- Editorial assistant
- Insurance sales
- Legal assistant
- Word-processing specialist
- Sales (office equipment and supplies)
- Airline reservation agent
- Hotel and motel personnel
- Meeting planner
- Production assistant (TV, cable, or radio)
- Publicity assistant
- Public-relations assistant
- Owner, typing or word-processing business
- Owner, secretarial or word-processing training institution
- Medical assistant
- Bill collection worker
- Wholesale trade salesperson
- Library technician and assistant
- Computer typesetter
- Photographer
- Bookkeeper
- Insurance-claim representative
- Retail trade salesperson
- Court reporter
- Data-input specialist
- Purchasing agent
- Medical record clerk

TABLE 15
Careers Teachers Can Transfer To:

- Trainer (corporate or free-lance)
- Educational liaison for computer manufacturers
- Writer (educational material)
- International educational consultant
- Real-estate salesperson
- Business owner
- Salesperson (textbook publishing)
- Salesperson (office equipment for schools)
- Marketing representative
- Magazine sales (educational specialist)
- Consultant (educational television)
- Scriptwriter (educational films)
- Production staff (educational television)
- Educational specialist (museums)
- Career counselor
- Meeting planner
- Staff, educational professional association (i.e., National Education Association)
- Staff (union education staff)
- Convention liaison (hotel and convention centers)
- Travel consultant/tour leader—educational tours
- Public-relations specialist
- Insurance, group sales (schools, educational institutions)
- Actuary (for math teachers)
- Commercial artist and/or graphic designer (for art teachers)
- Free-lance aerobics teacher (for physical-education teachers)
- Editor, magazine (educational specialist)
- Purchasing agent (educational institution)
- Buyer, retailing (teachers have knowledge of the teenagers' or young people's market)
- Photographer
- Newspaper reporter (educational topics)
- Technical writer (science teachers)
- Management trainee (corporation)
- Publisher—educational books
- Fund-raiser
- Staff, corporate health-center/gyms (for physical education teachers)
- Research, corporations
- Owner (nursery, day care or secondary school)
- Owner (educational institution)

TABLE 16
Careers Social Workers Can Transfer To:

- Career counselor
- Free-lance writer (family, drug, alcohol, stress-management tapes, etc.)
- Management consultant
- Free-lance trainer (drug and alcohol, stress, etc.)
- Real-estate property manager (senior citizens' activities, etc.)
- Human-resource staffer
- Home/health aide registry
- Conference or meeting planner
- Owner (own clinical practice)
- Marketing researcher
- Staffer, professional association
- International consultant
- Instructor, colleges, graduate school or adult-education program
- Staffer, nonprofit agency
- Salesperson, nursing-home supplies
- Salesperson, hospital supplies
- Staffer, health-maintenance organization
- Marketing representative, health-maintenance organization.
- Staffer, large religious organization
- Administrator, senior citizens' residential center.
- Administrator, private drug or alcohol rehabilitation clinic
- Community-relations staffer, corporation
- Public-relations staffer, corporation
- Business owner
- Real-estate sales
- Representative, insurance sales (i.e., health insurance)
- Free-lance fund-raiser for community in nonprofit organizations

TABLE 17
Careers Nurses Can Transfer To:

- Pharmaceutical sales
- Staff, corporate health program
- Staff, corporate stress-management/reduction center
- Diet-management specialist—physician's office
- Owner, home/health aide registry
- Nurse practitioner
- Staff, health-maintenance organization
- Corporate—nurse consultant
- Staff (educational institution or union health office/program)
- Trainer (stress management, alcohol or drug abuse)
- Rape or crisis hotline staff
- Fund-raiser (specialty hospital and other health organizations)
- Staff, health-insurance companies
- Public-relations specialist (specializing in hospital and other health-maintenance programs)
- Real-estate sales
- Group insurance sales (health organizations)
- Insurance sales (specialty health benefits)
- Health educator
- Sex counselor
- Hospital and medical-supply sales
- Real-estate property management (design health and fitness activities for senior citizens)
- Owner (health-educational institution)
- Human-resources specialist (health organizations)
- Administrator (health professional educational institution)
- Pharmaceutical marketing specialist
- Director, nursing or medical program (corporate)
- Staff, employee-assistance program

TABLE 18
Careers Lawyers Can Transfer To:

- Meeting planner
- Owner, business, in any industry
- Fund-raiser
- Writer, legal topics (magazines and newspapers)
- Owner, or staff, lecture-management bureau
- Manager, health-maintenance organization
- Executive recruiter
- Trainer, in-house corporate, management-consulting firm or free-lancer
- Labor management arbitrator for unions or government agencies
- Special-events marketer
- Development attorney in real estate
- Staffer, professional association, i.e., American Bar Association
- Computer-law specialist, consultant, or business owner
- Mortgage broker
- Employee-leasing executive (acts as personnel department for firms that don't have the resources to handle the paperwork and overhead of hiring employees)
- Salesperson
- Marketing specialist
- Entertainment attorney
- Legal adviser to TV or movies
- Literary agent
- Script agent
- High-tech traffic manager (a rapidly growing area that utilizes skills in law, contract negotiation, and distribution. Makes sure products are shipped safely, swiftly, and cheaply. Many specialize in international markets)
- Real-estate sales
- Public relations
- Manager, entertainers
- Assembly person, congressperson
- Administrator, nonprofit agency or organization
- Teacher, college or law school
- Administrator, college or law school
- Financial consultant, brokerage firm
- Manager, corporation

TABLE 19
Careers Cosmetologists Can Transfer To:

- Staffer, professional association (beauty or fashion industry)
- Production assistant, beauty/fashion television show
- Marketing representative, fashion or beauty companies and manufacturers
- Public-relations representative, fashion or beauty companies or manufacturers or salons
- Photo stylist
- Salesperson, beauty-supply company or beauty-fashion manufacturer
- Buyer or assistant buyer, beauty products, retailing establishment
- Research assistant for manufacturer (beauty industry)
- Technician or technical supervisor (beauty manufacturer)
- Beauty editor (magazine)
- Beauty editorial assistant (magazine)
- Free-lance writer (magazines that specialize in beauty)
- Personnel counselor (employment agency specializing in placement in beauty or fashion industries)
- Color consultant
- Owner (own cosmetics line)
- Owner, beauty-supply house
- Owner, nail salon
- Staffer, spa
- Instructor, cosmetology school
- Trainer, i.e., "corporate dressing," "presentation skills," etc.
- Consultant, beauty manufacturer

CHAPTER 5

Designing Your Career-Changing Game Plan

In the preceding chapters you learned how to set goals, analyze your skills (paid and unpaid) and work accomplishments, determine the skills needed for your new position, and decide on the careers to which you could transfer your abilities. Now it's time to develop some surefire career-changing techniques: ways to design your own career-changing game plan.

Career changers tend to rely on established ways of looking for a job: want ads, employment agencies or executive-search firms, and state employment agencies. Some job seekers are successful using these methods, but many are not.

I'm sure you've often heard the saying, "If you want something done right, do it yourself." This is certainly true when you want to change careers! Don't rely on others to find a better job for you—do most of the work yourself and you will probably be far happier with the results.

Donna Wilson (not her real name), who was a social worker and is now a business executive, took control of her career-changing campaign and ended up in the per-

fect spot for her. Several years ago she took a sabbatical from her job, but as her leave drew to an end, she felt strongly that social work was no longer for her. Putting security, pension, and benefits behind her, she decided to abandon the field.

She had read many career books during her leave and soon started eagerly putting some of their advice to work. The first thing this former social worker decided to do was target the industry and company she wanted to work for. She had always been intrigued by the advertising field. Another field that interested her was the communications industry.

After researching these two industries, she chose advertising. Donna Wilson decided to work for a large advertising agency, where better training opportunities might exist. She thoroughly investigated and selected the largest agency in the field. She read its annual report and dozens of magazine and newspaper articles about it. She soon had a grasp of the company's profits and losses, future growth prospects, and other pertinent factors.

But Wilson took her research one step further. She learned where this agency's employees spent many of their after-work hours: a restaurant several blocks from their office. This savvy career-changer spent many hours at the restaurant, chatting with employees of her future company. This type of "research" paid off handsomely, for she learned many tips that would help her in her interview.

Wilson had her heart set on working for this particular agency, but she had no business experience. So she tucked her concerns aside and began her next career-changing phase—networking by joining various women's organizations. Through one organization, she learned of a special program for women like herself who wanted to work in advertising but had no former experience. One of the program's participating agencies was the one where Wilson wanted a job.

She applied, and put her career-changing research to work. At one of the interviews, she used some of the "insider" information she had picked up. She was told that her prospective employer loves highly motivated employees. When the interviewer asked, "What quality would best describe you?" she replied in her most enthusiastic manner: "Well, I'm highly motivated to get the job done. My last assignment was to put together an extensive recruiting effort. I spent long hours and a great deal of energy to complete the assignment. By motivating my team of fellow social workers, we performed in an exemplary way."

This potential advertising executive felt that she knew the agency as well as any outsider could, and continuously displayed this knowledge during interviews. One tidbit of information that really helped was her knowledge of the different positions within the agency. She selected the one which most interested her: copywriter.

So when one interviewer asked what position she would like, Wilson answered, "associate copywriter." Knowing her future position further helped impress the interviewer. Many job applicants have no idea of what they want to do in a company or where they want to work.

Wilson received the position, and has since had several promotions. Other career-changing hopefuls weren't as successful as Donna Wilson. One is an associate of mine who is a teacher and also wanted to be accepted into the advertising program. She did little or no industry research and knew very little about her targeted company. On her way to an interview with an agency, she stopped by my office for an analysis of her résumé and to learn a few things to say. It was clear she knew little about the company, but I told her to stress strengths like people-management skills learned from teaching. But we had limited time to explore what that really consisted of.

At the interview, she proudly stressed her people-management skills, only to be pressed about it by the interviewer. She didn't fully explain what she meant, and ultimately didn't get the job.

The stories of Wilson and my associate show the differences in approach. Wilson was thorough; my associate was not. Remember, if you put a great deal into something, you'll get a great deal out of it. If you put little into something, you'll get little out.

Now let's start helping you put some substance into your career-change strategy. You are going to learn to design your own career-changing game plan and help your dreams come true.

First, like Wilson, you must decide what you really want to do. Some of you know or have an idea. Others of you are really stumped. If you don't know, try reviewing your skills list from Chapter 2.

Ask yourself: Is there any position that interests me? Try to write down one or two careers that interest you. Are there any particular skills that you would like to use in a new career? Try to get in touch with something that really interests you. Forget about your doubts right now. Just use one or two possible careers with which to begin. Eventually you will become more definite.

If you're really stumped on deciding what you want to do, a career counselor can help. For a list of career counselors in your area contact the National Board for Certified Counselors, 5999 Stevenson Avenue, Suite 402, Alexandria, VA 22304. Their phone number is 703-461-6222.

COMPANY AND INDUSTRY SELECTION

Once you've decided on one or two career areas, it's time to do some research. Most career fields have professional associations. One function of these associations is to dispense information to those interested in entering the field. Many of them will send you career information for free or for a small fee. Write them and request this information. To locate the professional association in your field, ask your librarian for the *Encyclopedia of Associations* (Gale Research) or the *National Trade and Professional Associations of the United States and Canada and Labor Unions* (Garrett Press, Garrett Park, Maryland). Appendix C is a list of selected professional associations.

You will be surprised at the usefulness of some of the material you receive from the associations. Information might include lists of skills needed for your future career, or descriptions of a variety of positions within each area. However, you should not stop your investigations here. You should also ask your librarian to help you locate books, magazines, and newspaper articles about your field: for example, the *Occupational Outlook Handbook* (U.S. Department of Labor, Bureau of Labor Statistics) contains very helpful material.

After you have researched your targeted career areas, it is now time to study your future industry or industries. In Table 20 you will find a list of possible industries. What do you know about each one? Which one or two are most appealing?

TABLE 20
Selected List of Industries

• Advertising	• Fashion	• Publishing
• Agriculture	• Finance	• Recording
• Auto	• Health care	• Retailing
• Banking	• Hotel and motel	• Service
• Communications	• Legal services	• Travel
• Computer	• Manufacturing	• Telecommunications
• Construction	• Magazine publishing	
• Cosmetics and beauty	• Precision production	

Remember that industries have "personalities." Do you want to work for a conservative, fashionable, fast-paced, research-oriented, or other type of industry? You must have a good personality match with the industry in which you will work. For example, if you are very shy and don't like to talk to people, you probably won't want to work in the service industry, where there is generally considerable people contact.

A person who can't make deadlines and doesn't like a fast-paced environment probably wouldn't like magazine publishing. Someone who is machine-phobic probably wouldn't adjust well to the computer industry. If you don't like dealing with money or facts and figures, finance probably won't suit you.

Bear in mind that word-processing specialists, administrative assistants, salespersons, accountants, legal assistants, public-relations specialists, computer programmers, human-resources specialists, marketing representatives, and managers can work in a wide variety of industries. For example, if you are an administrative assistant and would love a fast-paced, deadline-oriented environment, you might want to move to public relations or magazine publishing. Or if you are an accountant who loves the glamour and excitement of films, you might find a place in the film industry.

Be careful to select your industry wisely. Many people who think they're unhappy with their jobs are actually not dissatisfied with their jobs, but with the entire industry in which they work.

After you have done your industry selection, it's time to select your company. Companies come in all sizes: large, medium-large, medium, or small. One of the biggest mistakes most job seekers make is applying only at the large, better-known places. While it is fine to list the giants among those places where you would like to work, also include some medium-large, medium, and small companies: you could find more interesting career opportunities and even employers more receptive to career changers.

The best way to start your company research is to select one or two. Find out as much as you can about them. Contact the public-relations department of each company and request the latest annual report. It should be full of information about the company. You should be able to learn what the company does, how it is ranked in its industry, what its profits or losses were last year. Is it a multinational? If so, what countries is it in? What are its products or services? Its future products? Its plans for expansion or relocations?

There may be books, magazines, and newspaper articles about your future company. Ask your librarian for them. You may find material like the *F & S Index of Corporations and Industries* helpful. A good book that profiles details about some companies is *The 100 Best Companies to Work for in America*, by Robert Levering, Milton Moskowitz, and Michael Katz (Signet Paperback, 1987).

There are also directories like *Dun & Bradstreet's Reference Book of Corporate Managements*, which contains profiles of company executives. Through more research, you may want to find out in what departments the company's top executives began. Take a look at how they made their climb and how long it took.

Another important thing to find out about a firm is its code of ethics—things like dress requirements, expected employee behavior, or the "perfect" employee profile. At some companies everyone is expected to dress pretty much the same way. If you find that your would-be employer likes its people in charcoal-gray or navy-blue suits, and you're a more casual dresser, you might have to renew your wardrobe. Or perhaps the employees are expected to be "company men and women" who live and breathe The Company. Think about whether you want to or could live this way.

Make sure you understand the company's "corporate culture." Ask yourself if you are willing to accept, to embrace it. If not, look elsewhere. Be realistic. Accept what you can. What you can't, don't. There are literally thousands of companies in America from which to choose, so pick one that really suits you.

If you are a woman, a black person, or of another racial or ethnic minority, make sure the company has women or minorities in positions of authority. What is its record on affirmative action? After all, you want to work where you'll have career flexibility and can go as far as your abilities permit.

Other things to ask yourself about your future company are whether the benefits, pensions, or profit-sharing programs are industry competitive. Are the employees well treated? Is the company in good financial condition? Is it going to be taken over? Have there been massive layoffs or a general belt-tightening?

You may want to know if there are innovative programs. Does the firm have flexible hours? Are there on-site day-care centers? If these programs are important to you, search them out.

Two of the biggest factors in selecting a company may be your career mobility and salary. Find out if employees are moved along rapidly or tend to remain put for too long. Are salaries competitive? Remember that many professional associations do annual salary surveys of their members. Contact the association in your field.

FACT-FINDING INTERVIEWS

After you have completed the research part of your career homework, it's now time to interview people in your future field. These are called fact-finding interviews. Talking to people who know about your intended field will give you invaluable information and will help you round out your knowledge.

Many people are apprehensive about approaching those in higher positions. Don't be! Most people love to talk about themselves and their work, and since the object of these interviews is information and not a job, they will usually be glad to talk with you.

You will want to find out what people do in the field, the education and training needed, what skills are required, salary ranges, and how a career changer can break into the field. If you talk to several people in your intended career area, imagine the wide range of information you will obtain.

An ex-instructor wanted to become a consultant teaching top banking executives how to better communicate. He went on more than one hundred fact-finding interviews. By the time he had his last interview with a bank president, he had plenty of information about what he wanted to do. In fact, he presented the president with a proposal on how to better train his own executives in communication. As a result, this career changer received a contract to work with the bank's executives and went on to get more work from other banks.

So begin by going on at least one fact-finding interview. To help master your anxiety, consider the experience of one of my former students. She was sure that no one in a responsible position would talk to her, but she arranged an interview with a woman in a high position in public relations. Because this woman was impressed with my former student's skills and abilities, she recommended her for a job with another company—and my student became another successful career changer.

Sometimes you can look in your own backyard for people to interview. Some clients who worked in hospitals wanted to become respiratory therapists. I was surprised to learn that they hadn't even talked to the respiratory therapists at their own hospitals. They could have received a wealth of useful information from the therapists, and *did* once they approached them.

Whom do you know to interview? Look at your church or religious organization's members. What about friends, associates, or relatives? What about fellow employees? Suppose you want to become a computer programmer. Is there a programmer at your company or organization?

First, set up an interview with someone you know. Ask each person you interview for a referral, which will enable you to gain access to the next person. Then ask that person for a referral, and so on.

After each fact-finding interview, be sure to write a thank-you note. Say how much you enjoyed the meeting and how useful the information was. And make sure to let the person know how you are progressing in your efforts to change careers.

NETWORKING

Networking is an important component of career changing. You've already begun to establish a network through your fact-finding interviews. Now you are ready to build on it. Go where people with similar career goals and aspirations meet. Join professional associations. Many associations permit newcomers or nonmembers to attend local chapter meetings, where you can get priceless information and job leads.

Some professional associations allow nonmembers to attend their annual conferences or conventions. By attending, you will be able to make valuable contacts with people from all over the country. Some conventions or conferences also attract company recruiters who are looking to hire. Since recruiters may be looking for experienced people, you may not land a position this way, but use these opportunities to introduce yourself to them, learn about their hiring needs, and then periodically keep in touch with them.

WANT ADS, EMPLOYMENT AGENCIES AND EXECUTIVE-SEARCH FIRMS

Want Ads: Now that you've done your intensive career homework, like millions of career changers as the next step you'll probably pick up the wants ads and see what's available. This is fine and good, but be aware of the pitfalls!

Many want ads are "blind"—meaning that someone out there wants to collect résumés, but there isn't necessarily a position open. Why would someone pay for an ad for a nonexistent job? Some employment agencies do this to collect résumés for future use. There are many reasons. Let's say an agency knows that a company will have a future need for fifty word-processors. The agency might place the ad to find out how much talent is on the market. Meanwhile you've gone to the trouble to answer the ad and are frustrated that no one has contacted you.

Want ads are placed by a variety of people for a variety of reasons, so don't ever assume that all of them are legitimate. I once thought

I knew all of the possible reasons people place want ads. Then one day a newspaper article caught my eye. It seems that a man wanted to drop out of the rat-race corporate life and take on a new identity. He was an engineer, so he cleverly placed an ad that claimed to offer work in this field. Unsuspecting persons sent in their résumés. The engineer used one of them to look for a job and to begin a new life with a new identity.

A client of mine once answered an ad. She was cautious about replying to ads that gave only box numbers—blind ads. But this one bore a company name and an address. So how could there be a problem? Weeks passed and she didn't hear anything. My client was certain that her credentials were perfect for the job, and she couldn't understand the silence. She decided to look up the company name in the phone book. The company didn't exist. Now someone out there has her résumé and she has no idea who it is or what they are using it for.

Be careful when you answer want ads! My advice is to use them as one, but only one, method of looking for a job. Send your résumé only to a company after you have checked that is legitimate.

Employment Agencies and Executive-Search Firms: Some of these are great; others aren't beneficial to career changers. These firms obviously want to find the best, most experienced candidates for their client companies, so you'll have the problem of convincing them that you can handle the work required in a new, untried (in their view) career area.

These agencies and companies generally look very narrowly at an applicant's qualifications and training. For instance, a company client might want an agency to find a public-relations specialist with five years' ex-

perience. You've done PR work for a community group for five years, but it was on a volunteer basis. Your paid work was that of a secretary. Do you think the agency would consider you among its top candidates? Probably not. For them you are a secretary, nothing more.

It would be much easier for them to present to their client a public-relations specialist with five years of corporate experience. As a president of an executive-search firm told me, "We try to get people who are doing well in their careers but who may want better opportunities in the same field—just with another company."

Another problem that is particular with employment agencies is that they want many well-educated women who are career changers to accept secretarial positions. Unfortunately, many of these women think that the secretarial jobs will be stepping-stones: they can land better positions later. Don't fall into this trap. I've seen too many women accept "temporary" secretarial positions and be stuck there ten years later. *Consider only those positions for which you are qualified.*

This doesn't mean you should avoid employment agencies and/or executive-search firms. Just be selective. Understand that not all of them will be able to steer you to the job of your choice. Some will not even be interested in working with you. Some may put your name on a computer list and leave it there.

DESIGNING YOUR OWN JOB-SEARCH CAMPAIGN

Although career changers can use the traditional ways of looking for a job, designing your own job-search campaign will probably be more effective. Do as Donna Wilson did—

use the nontraditional job-search methods described in this chapter.

Determine what you want to do, research your future career area, select one or two industries where you want to work, choose one or two companies that appeal to you, and thoroughly investigate them. Go out on fact-finding interviews and network. In the last phase of your job search, you will find the person who can actually hire you and dazzle him or her with your skills, abilities, training, and talent.

Does designing your job-search campaign make a difference? Yes! Once I was looking for a job. Each Sunday I would go through that dreary process of searching the want ads for a suitable position. When I found one or two that were interesting, I sent résumés and cover letters. One or two employers contacted me, but interviews with them led nowhere.

So I finally decided to take matters into my own hands and designed a job search. I was a job developer trying to change careers and return to my former field of counseling. My first step was to decide where I wanted to work. The City University of New York (CUNY) is a large college system and paid counselors more than other schools. I decided wanted to work there.

Next, I determined in what department I wanted to work. Working with disadvantaged students was my preference, and the SEEK program was designed to help these students. I looked up the telephone numbers of the various colleges and called all the directors of the SEEK programs. "Are there any counseling positions available?" I asked. Two colleges had six positions available, and appointments for interviews were set up.

It was then time to intensify my career homework. I called everyone who even remotely knew something about CUNY, and my efforts paid off. I learned that there were social workers in most of the counseling positions in the SEEK programs. Since counselors and social workers are trained and approach counseling differently, I contacted all of my social worker friends to ask what to say and what to do in an interview with a social worker. They told me how to present myself as a typical social worker.

My interview at one of the colleges went very well. I was asked certain questions, and my answers were framed in typical social-worker jargon. The interviewer gave me the highest rating, and I was given the position.

How can you locate the person who can give you the job? First, determine who within the company or organization can hire you. Is it the president, vice president, or manager in charge of your future department? Do some research. There are directories like *Standard & Poor's Register of Corporations, Directors and Executives* or the *Corporate Address Book* (Perigee Books, 1987), by Michael Levine, which lists the names and addresses of many corporate executives.

Once you get the name, address, or telephone number of the person you want, try to reach him or her on the telephone. If you can't, send a "tailor-made" résumé and cover letter (see Chapter 6).

Personal referrals to your future boss can be helpful. Do you know anyone in the company who can refer you to this person? Your network contacts should be particularly helpful here.

Another good way to find potential hiring bosses is to look through professional or trade journals and magazines or newspaper articles. There can be a gold mine of information in them. For example, sometimes people discuss their company's present or future hiring needs. If you read about someone of interest, drop him or her a note.

One job seeker read an article about a woman in the computer field. She wrote to the woman thanking her for the information in the article and enclosed a copy of her résumé. Then she called the woman and arranged to have lunch. Later, when the woman needed someone to do a huge freelance assignment, she contacted and hired this resourceful job seeker.

In the next chapter you will learn how to write a résumé and cover letter that will get you an interview. Once you locate the person who can hire you, this will help you convince her or him that you are the perfect candidate.

CHAPTER 6

The Tailor-Made Résumé and Cover Letter

Now that you have targeted your future employer, you must dazzle this person with your skills. The best way to do this is by writing a dynamic résumé: it's the career changer's most important tool, and can make or break your chances for a successful change.

To help you write your résumé, begin by writing down essentials about your work history and educational background. Look at Table 21, the résumé-analysis chart. Fill in the answers and you are ready to begin creating your own résumé.

Most career changers think that there is only one type of résumé—the *chronological*, in which you list your work history and educational background in reverse chronological order (last job and school first). There are, however, two other types that may better serve the career changer—the *functional* and the *combination* résumés (see Tables 23 and 24).

First let's take a look at the chronological résumé. It should be used by those who want a similar position or a position above theirs. For example, if you are a salesperson and

want another sales position, you should use the chronological résumé; or if you are a salesperson who wants to become a sales manager.

But most career changers shouldn't use the chronological résumé. Why? It will highlight only what you are *currently* doing and what you did in *past jobs*. Your aim is to highlight what you *want* to be doing—and convince an employer that you can.

Table 22 is an example of a typical *chronological* résumé. It shows that Reesa Lindstrum is a payroll assistant. She began her work experience with this company and now seeks a similar position or one higher at another company. Her résumé is tailored to the position or positions she seeks. Lindstrum's résumé is also *results-oriented*, which means it emphasizes the results of the work done. For example, you may be a salesperson, but what makes you different from other salespeople? Review your work accomplishments and write, for example: "Increased sales for division by 50% in one quarter." Now that's impressive!

Now let's look at the résumés that are best

53

T A B L E 21
Résumé Analysis

1. What is your targeted position?
_____

2. What type of company do you want to work for, i.e., large, medium-large, medium, small?___

3. Where is it located? (city, state, country, etc.)
_____

4. What skills are needed for your future position?
_____
_____
_____
_____
_____
_____

5. What training is needed for your future position?
_____
_____

6. What prior work experience is needed?
_____
_____
_____

7. What qualities will give you the edge for the position?
_____
_____
_____

8. What work accomplishments do you have?
_____
_____
_____
_____

9. Write down all of your paid work positions.
a. Last or present position:_____
_____

b. Next positions:
_____
_____
_____
_____
_____

10. Write down all of your nonpaid work experience.
a. Last or present nonpaid position:
_____

b. Next nonpaid work positions:
_____
_____
_____

11. What are the educational institutions that you attended?
a. Last or present institution:
_____

b. Next institution:
_____
_____
_____

12. Have you taken any special courses at work, through your union, professional association, etc.? If so, which ones?
_____
_____
_____

13. Do you have any special skills, i.e., typing, word processing, languages? What are they?
_____
_____
_____

14. Have you received any awards or honors in your field? What are they?
_____
_____
_____

15. Do you belong to any professional associations or groups that are associated with your field? What are they?
_____
_____
_____

suited for career changers: *functional* and *combination* résumés. These allow the career changer to pinpoint skills needed for a particular career. The functional résumé highlights skills needed for a particular job. The combination résumé highlights skills and also includes chronological work and educational information. It is a combination of the functional and chronological résumés. With either of these résumés, you can show a potential employer that your skills are tailor-made for the position. In addition, each can camouflage an unsteady work history.

In Table 23, Laura Grant wants to change careers from a teacher to a job developer. A job developer finds jobs for unemployed or hard-to-place clients of nonprofit agencies. She has worked as a job developer twice: at the North Corridor Manpower Center, and at the Macon County Drug and Alcohol Department. The problem is that she held these jobs for only six months each.

In her fourteen years in the work force, Laura has had a hodgepodge of positions, including teaching at a high school, counseling, job developing, public relations, and sales. Now she has a chance to land a lucrative senior job-developer's position with a state agency. A chronological résumé would do two things: clearly show that she has only a short period of work experience as a job developer and make her look like a chronic job-hopper.

She rightly chose the functional résumé. It shows that although she was in each job-development position for only six months, she contributed a great deal, had a high placement rate of clients, and clearly knows the ins and outs of that field.

Laura put herself in the place of her future employer and asked, "If I were hiring a job developer, what would I want that person to have in terms of skills, experience, education, and training?" She started writing her functional résumé by determining the most important skill needed to be a job developer, which is . . . job development! And this becomes her first major skill area.

Laura chose career development as the second major skill area. Since job developers need to know the ins and outs of various careers—salaries, duties, training, and so on—and have—or should have—contacts in the work world, she demonstrates knowledge in this area. She points out that she has given workshops on a variety of career subjects for different organizations.

The third major skill area this career changer chose is counseling. Job developers' clients are generally unemployed and often need referrals to government agencies for food stamps, medical care, or other vital services. So a good job developer is also a good counselor.

With the major skill areas in place, Laura then made her résumé results-oriented. In the second paragraph, for example, Laura has written, "100% of job-club participants were placed with private and not-for profit companies." This impressive placement statistic alone would probably make any employer want her. Note that she strategically places statistics or work accomplishments throughout her résumé.

Laura completes her résumé with her educational training and awards, again taking care to select accomplishments that highlight her ability to do job developing.

In the combination résumé (Table 24), Anna Reeves wants to change from an associate administrator for a state department of education to a training administrator or manager at a corporation. Originally her résumé was a jumbled mixture that included teach-

TABLE 22
Chronological Résumé

REESA LINDSTRUM
845 Goldenrod Pond
Richmond, Virginia 37213
(804) 555–4380
(804) 555–6684

WORK EXPERIENCE
June 1986–Present

HLM Company, Richmond, Virginia

Payroll Assistant—
In charge of preparing monthly payroll (25,000)
for 200 professional and blue-collar workers.
Responsible for collecting timesheets and W-4s and
for logging information into computerized payroll
system.

Devised system to increase efficiency of payroll
calculations: introduced data-processing system
that has saved company *$27,000* annually.

Handle payroll deductions. Dispatch expense
accounts to personnel. Process insurance claims for
disability, union, Workmen's compensation, Blue
Cross/Blue Shield, Major Medical and
unemployment insurance.

EDUCATION
1984–1986

Ridgewood Community College, Mt. San Angelo,
Virginia

Received Associate of Arts Degree in Accounting.

SPECIAL SKILLS

Computer Programs: Cobol, Basic, Lotus 1-2-3.
Bilingual (Spanish/English).

REFERENCES   Furnished Upon Request.

ing, sales, and international work. Like so many career changers, she included every one of her many positions in the "work-experience" part of her résumé, and thus looked like a confused job-hopper.

After some career counseling, Reeves realized that her major work for the past six years had been in training and training administration. Although her last two titles were associate administrator and assistant administrator, her job duties were actually those of a training administrator and manager.

With that in mind, she wrote a combination résumé to accurately reflect her duties. This résumé allowed her to emphasize her major skill areas—training administration/management. She was also able to use chronological work information because her work history complements her skills.

By contrast, a person like Grant (in Table 23) would harm herself by using the combination résumé. Her chronological work history would highlight the short stints in job-developing positions.

Like Grant and Reeves, most career changers will want to use either the functional or the combination résumé. So: Decide what you want to do and determine what are the skills needed for the position and the matching skills that you possess. And don't forget to make your résumé results-oriented.

THE TAILOR-MADE COVER LETTER

Every career changer also needs a tailor-made cover letter. This letter should be addressed to each prospective employer and "tailored" to the position in mind. It must be grammatically correct, carefully typed, and be on your best stationery.

Let's see how to write an effective cover letter.

There are several types. The first type is the "referral" letter, which you send to someone referred by a friend or associate. Begin by explaining who referred you and what kind of job you want. For example:

Dear Mr. Jones:

Ms. Nancy Drew, of the National Association of Computer Technicians, referred me to you. She indicated that you have several Computer Technician III positions available in your Research and Development Department.

Another type of cover letter is the "answer to a want ad/job posting" type. It should also be addressed to whoever is hiring. Most job postings give the name of the person who is doing the hiring. But, you may be thinking, many want ads don't do this. In that case phone the company and ask who is in charge of hiring for the job you want.

The third type of cover letter is written to someone you've read about in a trade or professional journal, or perhaps in a general-interest or women's magazine. Some astute job seekers constantly read publications, looking for potential employers who have been written up in them for some reason or other. An article in a professional or trade journal could hint at certain hiring needs. Let's say for example that you've come across an article about a manager who will be adding over 100 people to her firm's training staff over the next few years. If this company is of interest to you, you could send her your résumé and cover letter.

Now let's look at the sample cover letter in Table 25. Agnes Woods has read an article about Jane Tyler in *Personnel Today* magazine and has written to her expressing interest in a

TABLE 23

Functional Résumé

LAURA GRANT
85 Melrose Lane
Shawnee Mission, Kansas 03671
(602) 555—0634—Residence
(602) 555—8899—Business

MAJOR SKILL AREAS

JOB DEVELOPMENT

Supervised job-development team for North Corridor Manpower Center. Responsible for the job-development needs and placing of 300 trainees into secretarial, entry-level computer, clerical, and word-processing positions. Designed and led videotaped interview sessions, job-hunting, and résumé-writing workshops. Have present placement rate of 95% of participants into jobs.

Ran job clubs for North Corridor Manpower Center's social-service aides. Job-club procedures included morning sessions on job-hunting techniques and afternoon sessions on interviews and/or "fact-finding" interviews. 100% of job-club participants were placed with private and not-for-profit companies. Wrote bimonthly newsletter on job opportunities. Resulted in 60% of participants placed through this procedure.

Did job development as rehabilitation vocational counselor for Macon County Drug and Alcohol Department. Held job-search sessions on interviewing techniques and résumé writing for ex-drug and ex-alcoholic clients. Placed 75% of clients in jobs with county and nonprofit organizations.

Consultant to Lanview Career Centers on job-developing procedures and job-search techniques.

Did vocational counseling and job development for Caldwell Adult Education Center. Placed students with G.E.D. program into positions at Catholic Hospital. 90% of clients were placed.

CAREER DEVELOPMENT

Have given seminars on career development: skill building and assessment for homemaker and volunteer workers; résumé and cover-letter writing; interviewing techniques; salary and promotion negotiations and corporate survival.

Major career workshops have been held at Trinity Women's Center; Shawnee Mission Junior College; The University of Arkansas; Office of the Governor (State of Kansas); Kansas State Department of Civil Services (Women's Conference); Westwood Women's Center; Shawnee Mission Board of Education; St. Mary's School (Career Conference); Melrose Library; Shawnee Mission Library's Educational and Career Informational Center; Linwood Business School; Women in Communications Conference; Keyes Business Business Academy and others.

COUNSELING

Provided personal counseling to approximately 70 adults per term at Loeb's Vocational Center. Designed program to increase students' awareness of academic and career issues. Instituted weekly "rap" sessions for clients.

Developed and implemented "Resource Network System" for counselors and other staff at Loeb to maintain referral lists of agencies and other resources for clients. "System" serviced 500 clients.

Provided academic and personal counseling to 80 teenagers in Macon County Drug Prevention Program. 43% of clients remained drug-free for twelve months or more.

EDUCATION

1975–1978	Indiana State University, Terre Haute, Indiana. Received Master's degree in Education.
1971–1975	Carlowe College, Pittsburgh, Pennsylvania. Awarded Bachelor of Arts degree in Psychology.

SPECIAL TRAINING

1980	Received certificate in Drug and Alcohol Therapy from Crainkin Institute, Shawnee Mission, Kansas.
1982	Received certificate for attending workshop "Innovations in Job Development" at the University of Kansas.
1984	Completed course "Computers for Job Developers" at the University of Kansas.
1986	Awarded certificate for completion of course "Grant-Proposal Writing" at the University of Kansas.
1987	Received third-place prize for article "Job Needs of Ex-Drug and Alcohol Teens" in competition given by the National Association of Professionals in Drug and Alcohol Programs.

REFERENCES

Will be furnished upon request.

training position. In the first paragraph she congratulates Tyler on the article. Next, she indicates a knowledge of Tyler's future personnel needs, as indicated in the article.

In the third paragraph Agnes talks about her background and *highlights only the training work*. For more details, the prospective employer can refer to her résumé.

In the last paragraph Agnes says that she will call Tyler in two weeks to set up an appointment. She does this to make sure that the employer will be expecting her call, and to eliminate the anxiety caused by waiting that affects most job seekers.

Have fun writing your tailor-made résumé and cover letter! If done correctly, these two tools will help propel you to success!

Now let's look at Table 26 for some résumé do's and don'ts.

TABLE 24
Combination Résumé

Anna Reeves
380 North Street
Englewood, New Jersey 43356
(212) 555-7980—Office
(201) 555-2020—Home

MAJOR SKILL AREAS

TRAINING ADMINISTRATION/MANAGEMENT

Responsible for the establishment and management of a $6.5 million Career and Education Training Program at the State of New Jersey Department of Education for over 60,000 participants. Under directorship, program has grown from one to twenty-five educational centers in New Brunswick, Newark, Trenton and Parsippany. Responsible for hiring and supervision of one Assistant Administrator, one Assistant to the Administrator, five coordinators, 25 site coordinators and 75 site staff personnel.

Responsible for the planning, coordinating, and day-to-day managing of program. In charge of all promotion and advertising to increase trainee participation. As a result of extensive promotional and advertising activities, program participation has increased from 75 to 20,000 trainees per cycle. Responsible for the formulation of training policies and procedures. Coordinate and develop all training materials.

As Assistant Administrator for Career Development Projects at the State of New Jersey Department of Education was responsible for coordination of programs, i.e., computer technician trainee, licensed practical nurses' training program, etc. Over 20,000 employees participated in programs. Was responsible for writing proposals and cost-effective budgets.

MAJOR WORK EXPERIENCE

August 1984 to Present	State of New Jersey, Department of Education Trenton, New Jersey
	Associate Administrator
December 1980 to August 1984	*Assistant Administrator*

EDUCATION

1974 to 1976	Ohio State University, Columbus, Ohio Received Master of Arts in Curriculum Development.
1969 to 1973	Howard University, Washington, D.C. Received Bachelor of Arts in History.

References furnished upon request.

TABLE 25
Cover Letter

1811 Post Road
Columbus, Ohio 48722
January 9, 1990

Ms. Jane Tyler
Manager, Human Resources Division
Teleton Inc.
490 Hanna Drive
Newark, Ohio 47301

Dear Ms. Tyler:

Congratulations on your article in Personnel Today. I found it very informative and helpful.

I was particularly interested in your statements concerning the future personnel needs of your training division. As you explained in the article, your division will need more than 100 training specialists in the next year and a half.

My background in training and human resources may be particularly suitable for your division. My experience includes:

—Over ten years of free-lance training for organizations like Girl Scouts of America, Volunteers of America, the Board of Education (Columbus, Ohio), Ohio State University, and Case Western Reserve University.

—The completion of four courses ("Developing Training Techniques I and II," "Marketing Yourself as a Trainer," and "Creating Dynamic Training Leadership Qualities") at the National School of Training.

—Over twelve years of training and training curriculum development at the Board of Education (Columbus, Ohio).

Your division's work sounds very innovative and challenging. I would very much like to discuss becoming a member of your team. For your reference, I have enclosed a copy of my résumé.

I will call you in two weeks to set up an appointment. Or I can be reached at (614) 555-9867.

Sincerely,

Agnes Woods

TABLE 26
Résumé Do's and Don'ts

Do's

- Think of your résumé as a "60 Second Commercial." Include only *relevant information* to describe your work and educational experiences. Think of the average television commercial. A company could probably write or say a great deal more about its product, but doesn't. It uses only the best, *attention-grabbing phrases* in its commercial. You should think of your résumé in much the same way.

- Think of your job duties instead of job title when writing a résumé.

- Tailor or gear your résumé toward the position that you want. In describing your job duties, use action words like advocate, communicate, detail, deliver, demonstrate, display, draw, edit, evaluate, and organize.

- Use the functional or combination résumé when changing careers.

- Use the correct employment dates.

- Put yourself in the place of the employer. What does he or she want in an employee?

- Explain the results of your work by using work accomplishments on your résumé.

- Use a one- or two-page résumé. A résumé isn't an autobiography.

- Invest in having your résumé typeset or done on a word-processing machine.

- Invest in good paper such as 100% rag, parchment, or linen.

Don'ts

- Don't list every position you've had since high school. List only those that are *relevant* to the position you want.

- Don't lie on your résumé.

- Don't state salaries or salary history on your résumé.

- Don't list irrelevant information like health, weight, age, hobbies, or marital status.

- Don't list references on your résumé.

- Don't list the names of your supervisors.

- Don't describe your job duties and work accomplishments in whole sentences. For example, don't say, "I am responsible for the design of office equipment," but "Responsible for design of office equipment" or "Design office equipment."

- Don't let typos, spelling errors, or poor grammar appear on your résumé.

- Don't list a job objective unless it is specific, i.e., "Computer Programmer II position in large manufacturing company in the Midwest."

- Don't let your résumé imply, "I don't really care about getting this job."

CHAPTER 7

Rising to the Top of the Interview Game

Your résumé and cover letter should have opened doors for you to be invited for interviews in corporations or other organizations. Now you must sell yourself in person to your prospective employer.

It is now time to prepare for your interview. To do so, try to anticipate what will happen during it. Remember, your future boss wants to find the best person for the job. It's up to you to convince him or her that you are this person.

An employer will want to know that you have a basic understanding of the company and its purpose. Go back to your career homework notes. What does the company do? What are its present and future products? Was the company profitable last year? If not, what were its approximate losses? What are its future plans?

Review your notes from talks with networking sources. What did they say about the company? What inside information did *you* discover about your future company?

You must convince the employer that you can handle the work required for the position. Review the skills needed for it and matching skills you can transfer to your fu-

ture position (see Chapter 2). Have you performed this work in the past? What strengths do you have that will help you do the job? Is your future position a "line" one that directly contributes to sales and profits? Or is it a staff or support position?

What do you know about your future department? Why does it exist? How does it fit into the scheme of the company or organization?

What do you know about the interviewer? Is this person the boss or someone who is screening for the boss? Will you have to interview with more than one person? If so, will it be in a group situation? What is your interviewer's title? Her or his achievements or hobbies?

In preparation for your interview you should also include doing practice interviewing with a friend. Give the questions in Table 27 to a friend to quiz you. The questions are designed especially for the career changer. By answering each question, you should be prepared for any interview situation.

If you can, see how you might look in an interview. Some people videotape their practice interviews. If you work for a college or

TABLE 27
Sample Interview Questions

- What do you know about our company?
- Why did you choose our company?
- Tell me about yourself.
- What are your career goals?
- Where do you expect to be in your career within five years? Ten years?
- What are your educational goals?
- What future training do you plan in connection with your career goals?
- What are your lifetime goals?
- What do you know about the position I'm interviewing you for?
- What skills, experience, and training do you have that make you qualified for the job?
- What other positions have you had that qualify you for the position?
- What have you contributed to your past employers that saved the company time, money, or enhanced its image?
- How many promotions did you receive at your last or present company? Your next-to-last position? The one before that?
- Why were you given these promotions at your present or last company? Your next-to-last position? The one before that?
- How many raises were you given at your last position?
- Why were you given them?
- What did you learn in your last three positions?
- Do you like your job? Why?
- During your career, which position did you like best?
- What are you particularly good at in your present position? Why?
- What qualities have you exhibited in your present position? Your next-to-last position? The one before that?
- What were some of the shortcomings that you exhibited in your last position?
- Why do you want to change careers?
- What major strength do you feel you have that will make you a great manager?
- Have you any supervisory or administrative experience? Please tell me about it.
- What is your management style?
- How are your people-management skills? Can you give me one or two examples?
- How well do you communicate in writing and orally? Give me some examples of this.
- Can you meet deadlines? If so, give me an example.
- Give me an example of a decision you made that benefited your company.
- What would your boss say about you?
- If the people who work with you were to evaluate you, what would they say?
- What motivates you?
- How do you best motivate others?
- What professional associations do you belong to?
- What civic organizations do you belong to?
- What clubs do you belong to?
- What volunteer work do you do or have you done in the past?
- What awards or honors have you received?
- Have you ever received any fellowships? When? Why? What did you do?
- Have you written any articles for a professional journal, magazine, or newspaper? When? What were they about?
- Have you ever done consulting work? If so, why and for whom?
- What are your hobbies?
- What do you do in your spare time?
- Have you ever traveled? If so, where?
- Do you travel for your present or a past position? How much travel do you or did you do?
- Are you willing to travel for this position?
- If your career demanded it, would you be willing to relocate for advancement?
- Do you know about other countries and cultures? If so, which ones?
- What are your salary requirements?

organization that owns video equipment, arrange to have yourself taped. When you view your tape, pay attention to your body language, voice strength and quality, and ability to answer questions. Practice and try to improve yourself. Then retape your interview.

Another great way to prepare yourself for the interview is through visualization exercises. If you visualize a successful interview, its outcome will be successful. In order to do this visualization, set aside at least twenty minutes each day for ten days prior to the interview. Sit in a quiet spot and close your eyes. In the darkness, imagine the entire scene. See yourself getting up in the morning, dressing, and driving or riding the train or bus to the interview. Imagine the building where you are going. Enter it and ride the elevator to the right floor. See yourself being greeted by the receptionist. Remove your outer garments and sit down.

Next, see the interviewer. Reach for his or her hand and give him or her a strong handshake. Follow the interviewer into the office. Sit down. Visualize the interviewer liking you and asking many of the familiar questions you've prepared. See the interview ending on a positive note, with your being hired.

Some of you may look on this exercise as wasted time. But remember that many successful people use the technique to help them get what they want, or just to ease the jitters. Try it. You'll be amazed at how such a simple technique can help you to breeze through an interview. But it won't replace preparation, so you must use both.

Your last pre-interview preparation should focus on what to wear. In doing your career homework, you should have found out how the employees dress: conservative? chic? casual? Go back and talk with your networking sources. Ask people who work at the company or who are familiar with it. Your intention is to look as though you were already an employee. By looking the part, you will put the interviewer at ease and show that you already belong.

Remember that actors and actresses often dress like their future roles when they audition, which helps the casting people visualize them in the role. You can do the same in an interview: Looking the part will help you land the job.

Now let's discuss the different types of interview situations that you might encounter. Interviews used to be simple. There was an interviewer and a prospective employee. The interviewer usually asked all the questions, and the future employee responded only when asked, "Do you have any questions?" Usually the interviewee responded with questions concerning salary, vacation time, and benefits. Today things are much more sophisticated. There are many different types of interviews, and they are expected to be two-way conversations.

The first type of interview is the question and answer (Q and A). Here, the interviewer conducts things in a structured way. She or he wants to find out certain things about your likes and dislikes, skills, experience, training, and capabilities. Put your best foot forward, establish rapport with the interviewer, and stress your skills, training, and accomplishments. Make the interview a conversation instead of a one-sided talk given by the interviewer.

The next kind of interview is the unstructured type. Here, the interviewer usually begins with a question like this: "Tell me about yourself." He or she may say little else.

Once I interviewed to become a partner with a management-consulting firm. I was asked to talk about myself. I did so as enthusiastically and thoroughly as possible. I talked for about fifteen minutes, then stopped, but the interviewer said, "Please go on." I talked and talked about my past work, training, and skills until I felt I was running out of things to say. At one point I thought I'd have to fall back on childhood reminiscences, but I'm glad to say he stopped me before that happened. The interview was a success and I was offered a partnership with that company.

Make sure you have enough to say about yourself! Say it with confidence and be ready to carry the entire interview if it turns out to be the unstructured type.

Many businesses and organizations require prospective employees to interview with several people with whom they will work. These "successive" interviews can take place on one day, or you might be required to come in more than once. You will be required to impress your future co-workers, the boss, and maybe even the boss's boss. Just try to keep your energy level high enough to deal with all of them.

The group interview occurs where three or more of your future co-workers and possibly the boss interview you collectively. In this situation you must remain calm, relaxed, and ready to sell others on your abilities. I have found that there are usually one or two people in the group who will react to you in a negative, suspicious way. Try to ignore them and concentrate on the positive people.

When the interview is about to conclude, the interviewer may make you an offer. After salary has been brought up, it's time to put your career homework to work again. Bring to mind the salary surveys from the professional associations and the tips you received from fact-finding interviews. You should have a good idea of what the salary ranges are for your position.

Never, but never, accept the first offer. It is usually the lowest that an employer can give.

Repeat your list of accomplishments, skills, experience, and training. You may also want to tell the employer that you know what competitive salaries are for your future position. You might say, "That offer seems a bit low. It's my understanding that people with my level of expertise and experience command more."

Many job changers are afraid to negotiate for salaries, and often snap up the first offer. Some believe the employer would get mad and withdraw the job offer should they try to negotiate. Not true. Most employers will respect you for your firmness. If an employer really wants you, he or she will stretch the budget to accommodate your salary requirements. This does not mean of course that you can ask $50,000 for a job with a top salary of $20,000. Be realistic.

Sometimes career changers find it is impossible to make a big salary leap. Let's say you're making $20,000, and the pay scale for your new job is from $35,000 to $60,000. Even though you have the necessary skills and experience to command a mid-range salary—$45,000 to $50,000—many employers will be reluctant to give you such a hefty increase. This is just human nature, and only astute negotiation skills will enable you to overcome this hurdle. Try reading books on negotiation—there are many available in good bookstores. Or take a course at your local college or university.

After each interview, be sure to write a letter to the interviewer, thanking her or him for their time. The letter should also review points you made in the interview that you want this person to remember.

Remember: If you don't get the job, don't despair! Think of interviews as learning experiences. You will learn to handle yourself better after each interview.

Now look at Table 28 for some interview do's and don'ts.

TABLE 28
Interview Do's and Don'ts

Do's	Don'ts
• Always prepare yourself for the interview.	• Don't be nervous or jittery. Visualize your success.
• Be enthusiastic about the interview and your future company.	• Don't speak badly of your present or former employer.
• Know as much about the company as any "outsider" can know.	• Don't volunteer any negative information about yourself.
• Dress appropriately for the interview.	• Don't let the interview throw you into a tailspin.
• Be sincere.	• Don't discuss salary until it's brought up.
• Be honest.	
• Be positive.	
• Stress things like your skills, abilities, training, and work accomplishments.	
• Be on time.	
• Try to establish rapport with the interviewer.	
• Send a thank-you note to the interviewer.	

Now you have all the tools to make a successful career change and land your dream job. Since you'll spend nearly 100,000 hours in the work force, won't it be worth the effort and time to eventually work at something you love? You can do it! Just put in the time, imagine yourself a success, and it will happen. Happy job hunting!

APPENDIX A

Suggested Reading

Blanchard, Kenneth, and Spencer Johnson: *The One Minute Manager.* Berkley Books.

Bolles, Richard N.: *The Three Boxes of Life: And How to Get Out of Them.* Ten Speed Press.

——: *What Color Is Your Parachute?* Ten Speed Press.

Davis, George, and Glegg Watson: *Black Life in Corporate America.* Anchor Press/Doubleday.

Harragan, Betty Lehan: *Games Mother Never Taught You: Corporate Gamesmanship for Women.* Warner Books.

Jackson, Tom: *The Perfect Résumé.* Anchor Press/Doubleday.

Lathrop, Richard: *Who's Hiring Who.* Ten Speed Press.

Levine, Michael: *The Corporate Address Book: The Complete Directory to Who's Who and What's What in American Business Today.* Perigee Books.

Nivens, Beatryce: *The Black Woman's Career Guide.* Anchor Press/Doubleday.

——: *Careers for Women Without College Degrees.* McGraw-Hill.

Parker, Yana: *The Damn Good Résumé Guide.* Ten Speed Press.

Books on Positive Thinking

Goodman, Linda: *Star Signs.* St. Martin's Press.

Hill, Napoleon, and W. Clement Stone: *Success Through a Positive Mental Attitude.* Pocket Books.

——: *Think and Grow Rich.* Fawcett.

——: *You Can Work Your Own Miracles.* Fawcett.

Mandino, Og: *The Greatest Miracle in the World.* Bantam.

——: *The Greatest Salesman in the World.* Bantam.

——: *Mission Success.* Bantam.

Peale, Norman Vincent: *The Power of Positive Thinking.* Fawcett.

Ponder, Catherine: *The Dynamic Laws of Prosperity.* A Reward Book.

——: *The Prospering Power of Love.* Unity Books (Unity Village, Missouri).

Schuller, Robert H.: *Tough Times Never Last, but Tough People Do!* Bantam.

Schwartz, David: *The Magic of Thinking Big.* Cornerstone Library.

Shinn, Florence Scovel: *The Game of Life and How to Play It.* Devorss and Company.

_____: *The Secret Door to Success.* DeVorss.

APPENDIX B

Selected Professional Associations

Accounting
American Society of Women Accountants
National Headquarters
35 East Wacker Drive, Suite 2250
Chicago, IL 60601

National Association of Accountants
P.O. Box 433
10 Paragon Drive
Montval, NJ 07645

American Institute of Certified Public Accountants
  and Accreditation Council for Accountancy
1010 North Fairfax
Alexandria, VA 22314

Advertising
American Advertising Federation
1400 K Street, NW
Washington, DC 20005

American Association of Advertising Agencies
666 Third Avenue
New York, NY 10017

Banking
The National Association of Bank Women, Inc.
500 North Michigan, Suite 1400
Chicago, IL 60611

Communications
American Women in Radio and Television, Inc.
1101 Connecticut Avenue, NW
Suite 700
Washington, DC 20036

National Association of Broadcasters
1771 N Street, NW
Washington, DC 20036

Women in Communications, Inc.
P.O. Box 9561
Austin, TX 78766

Computers
Association for Systems Management
24587 Bagley Road
Cleveland, OH 44138

Data Processing Management Association
505 Busse Highway
Park Ridge, IL 60068

Cosmetology
National Hairdressers and Cosmetologists Association
3510 Olive Street
St. Louis, MO 63103

Court Reporting
National Shorthand Reporters Association
118 Park Street, SE
Vienna, VA 22180

Health Services
American Dental Assistants Association
666 North Lake Shore Drive, Suite 1130
Chicago, IL 60611

National Association of Dental Assistants
900 South Washington Street, Suite G13
Falls Church, VA 22046

Opticians Association of America
10341 Democracy Lane
P.O. Box 10110
Fairfax, VA 22030

National Association of Emergency Medical Technicians
P.O. Box 334
Newton Highlands, MA 02161

Hotel and Motel
American Hotel and Motel Association
888 Seventh Avenue
New York, NY 10019

Insurance
American Council of Life Insurance
1000 Pennsylvania Avenue
Washington, DC 20004

National Association of Insurance Women
P.O. Box 4410
Tulsa, OK 74159

Legal Assistants
National Association of Legal Assistants, Inc.
1420 South Utica
Tulsa, OK 74104

Personnel
American Society for Personnel Administration
606 North Washington Street
Alexandria, VA 22314

Photographers
Professional Photographers of America, Inc.
1090 Executive Way
Des Plaines, IL 60018

Public Relations
Public Relations Society of America, Inc.
845 Third Avenue
New York, NY 10022

Real Estate
National Association of Realtors
430 North Michigan Avenue
Chicago, IL 60611

Starting Your Own Business
Small Business Administration
1441 L Street, NW
Washington, DC 20416

American Women's Economic Development Corporation
60 East 42nd Street
New York, NY 10065

The *Practical Handbook Series* from Perigee to build the skills you need to get ahead!

TYPING

Typing for Beginners
by Betty Owen

Learn to type at your own speed with the same method taught at one of New York's most successful business schools. Written especially for the novice, *Typing for Beginners* includes scores of trouble-saving tips, specialized drills, speed and accuracy timings, and much more.

Touch Typing in Ten Lessons
by Ruth Ben'Ary

Over one million sold!

If you're in a hurry, here is the shortest complete home-study course in the fundamentals of touch typing. Taught for over forty years, the famous Ben'Ary method has proven successful for students of all ages and skill levels.

Shortcuts to Increase Your Typing Speed
by Elza Dinwiddie-Boyd

Sharpen your skills with this easy-to-follow series of exercises designed to improve dramatically your typing speed and accuracy without time-consuming drills. Includes a review of the differences between standard typewriter layout and keyboards used on computers and word processors.

COMMUNICATION

The Art of Letter Writing
by Lassor A. Blumenthal

Here's a straightforward guide to creating memorable letters of all kinds, from party invitations and condolence letters to letters of inquiry, job application letters, and letters of reference. Includes tips on spelling, grammar, and avoiding clichés.

Successful Business Writing
by Lassor A. Blumenthal

To advance in your career, you have to be able to organize your ideas and convey them logically and convincingly. Learn the principles of writing to fit every business need from résumés to proposals, memorandums, and speeches.

Successful Oral and Written Presentations
by Lassor A. Blumenthal

Lassor Blumenthal earns a six-figure income writing presentations for some of the world's largest and most demanding organizations. You too can learn to inform, excite, and persuade your audience, whether you're making a major sales pitch or a short report to the boss. Includes keys to organizing your thoughts, pointers to overcome nervousness, and attention-getting ways to use visual aids.

RÉSUMÉS

Over three million sold!

Job Résumés
by J. I. Biegeleisen

Here's how to write the résumé and prepare for the interview that will help you get the job you want. Includes 50 sample "sell yourself" résumés that are keyed to 225 alphabetically listed occupations so you can easily choose the résumé designed especially for the position you're looking for.

How to Write
Your First Professional Résumé
by J. I. Biegeleisen

How do you get a job when you have no experience, and how do you get experience when you can't get a job? In an easy question-and-answer format, Biegeleisen shows you how to write a résumé that turns your training, natural talents, and life experience into job qualifications. Includes over sixty sample résumés.

MEMORY

Success Through Better Memory
by Eric M. Bienstock, Ph.D.

In today's fast-paced, information-packed world, a good memory is essential to success. Now you can learn to remember names, faces, phone numbers—or anything else—in just fourteen days. Filled with illustrative examples, exercises, practical applications, and reviews.

Start building your future today with the *Practical Handbook Series* from Perigee—just call us toll-free at 1-800-631-8571, or fill out the coupon below and send your order to:

The Putnam Publishing Group
390 Murray Hill Parkway, Dept. B
East Rutherford, NJ 07073

The *Practical Handbook Series* is also available at your local bookstore or wherever paperbacks are sold.

			PRICE	
			U.S.	CANADA
_____	**Typing for Beginners**	399-51147-4	**$5.95**	**$8.50**
_____	**Touch Typing in Ten Lessons**	399-51529-1	**6.95**	**9.25**
_____	**Shortcuts to Increase Your Typing Speed**	399-51489-9	**5.95**	**8.50**
_____	**The Art of Letter Writing**	399-51174-1	**5.95**	**8.50**
_____	**Successful Business Writing**	399-51146-6	**6.95**	**9.25**
_____	**Successful Oral and Written Presentations**	399-51330-2	**6.95**	**9.25**
_____	**Job Résumés**	399-50822-8	**6.95**	**9.75**
_____	**How to Write Your First Professional Résumé**	399-51240-3	**6.95**	**9.75**
_____	**Success Through Better Memory**	399-51577-1	**7.95**	**10.50**

Subtotal $_____

*Postage & Handling: $1.00 for 1 book, $.25 for each additional book up to a maximum of $3.50

*Postage & Handling $_____
Sales Tax $_____
(CA, NJ, NY, PA)

Total Amount Due
Payable in U.S. Funds
(No cash orders accepted)

Please send me the titles I've checked above. Enclosed is my:

☐ check   ☐ money order

Please charge my

☐ Visa   ☐ MasterCard

Card # _____ Expiration date _____

Signature as on charge card _____

Name _____

Address _____

City _____ State _____ Zip _____

Please allow six weeks for delivery. Prices are subject to change without notice.